SHAMEFUL BEHAVIORS

Tim Delaney

University Press of America,® Inc.
Lanham · Boulder · New York · Toronto · Plymouth, UK

Copyright © 2008 by
University Press of America,® Inc.
4501 Forbes Boulevard
Suite 200
Lanham, Maryland 20706
UPA Acquisitions Department (301) 459-3366

Estover Road
Plymouth PL6 7PY
United Kingdom

Library of Congress Control Number: 2008925821
ISBN-13: 978-0-7618-4088-6 (paperback : alk. paper)
ISBN-10: 0-7618-4088-5 (paperback : alk. paper)
eISBN-13: 978-0-7618-4224-8
eISBN-10: 0-7618-4224-1

™
⊖ The paper used in this publication meets the minimum
requirements of American National Standard for Information
Sciences—Permanence of Paper for Printed Library Materials,
ANSI Z39.48—1984

Contents

List of Tables

Preface

Does it appear to you that more and more people are acting rudely and displaying poor etiquette in an increasing number of social situations? If you answered "yes," you are not alone in this belief. In fact, it appears as though there is a rising culture of shamelessness in the United States. That is, people are shamelessly engaging in behaviors that in the past would have brought embarrassment, shame, and a lower sense of self upon the perpetrator.

Shameful Behaviors presents a unique look at American culture based on the premise that not only is there a rising culture of shamelessness, there is also a corresponding rise in formal and informal resistance against this trend. These patterns of resistance come primarily in the form of formal and informal shamings.

Chapter 1, "The Growing Culture of Shamelessness," examines the role of culture in determining "proper" behavior and the appropriate sanctions that should be applied to those who violate the norms of society. A distinction between embarrassment and shame is also made, as it is argued that some behaviors may be embarrassing but not necessarily shameful.

Chapter 2 explores formal shamings, such as military court martials, judicial punishments, and workplace mobbings. Formal shamings are accompanied by degradation ceremonies. Degradation ceremonies are conducted by formal organizations and are designed to compromise the offenders' self-esteem and identity by stigmatizing, embarrassing, and shaming individuals. Informal shamings are discussed in chapter 3. Informal shamings are quasi-degradation ceremonies in that the perpetrators of these shamings are not formal organizations but, instead, regular people (e.g., friends, family members, sports teammates). This chapter also explores the idea that people actually find joy in shaming others for their shameful transgressions. Finding joy in other people's follies is an important aspect of the growing culture of shamelessness. However, the large number of informal shamings discussed would suggest that the culture of shamelessness is meeting resistance.

Perhaps the most intriguing aspect of shameful behaviors is the willingness of individuals to shame themselves. Chapter 4 explores this fascinating topic of self-shaming. Self-shaming may represent the epitome of the culture of shamelessness. Self-shaming involves such mild activities as playing donkey basketball, trying out for *American Idol* without having any singing talent, and posting intimate details on one's MySpace or Facebook page. In more serious cases, self-shaming may take the form of such unhealthy behaviors as self-hatred, self-mutilations, and eating disorders.

Chances are most people will find chapter 5 to be the most fascinating. In this chapter, the long-time tradition of drunk shamings is discussed. Drunk shamings incorporate many of the key elements of the culture of shamelessness. A drunk shaming occurs when people become too drunk to defend themselves from a private/public shaming. Drunk shamings are another type of quasi-degradation ceremony in that they are implemented by non-official personnel.

Often, the drunk person will have his or her picture taken which is then some-times placed on the Internet. Drunk shamings may involve drawing on the vic-tim's skin, putting objects on the victim (especially the exposed skin area), and rearranging the victim's body into embarrassing positions. (See my website for photo examples.)

In the final chapter, a brief review of the growing culture of shamelessness and the many forms of resistance against its continued growth is presented. Im-plications of the growing culture of shamelessness for the future will also be discussed.

An important underlining current throughout this book is the role of self-esteem on shameless and shameful behaviors. Original research on drunk sham-ings (see chapter 5) pays particularly close attention to the issues of self-esteem and self-identity.

It is intended that the reader of *Shameful Behaviors* will learn from, and be entertained by, the materials presented.

Acknowledgements

My initial interest in writing a book on shameful behaviors began with the original research I conducted with a former student, Patrick Tanzini, on the drunk shaming behaviors of college students. I would like to acknowledge Patrick's assistance with the drunk shaming data that appears in chapter five. Although the drunk shaming research was fascinating in its own right, it led me to many other ideas.

Gratitude must also be extended to Tim Madigan who reviewed early versions of this manuscript and to Beth Messana who assisted with the typesetting and formatting of the text. And, as always, special thanks to my continued inspiration, Christina.

Chapter 1

The Growing Culture of Shamelessness

"There is no shame in not knowing; the shame lies in not finding out"— Russian Proverb

During America's colonial era, people were modest, hard workers who went about their business without drawing attention to themselves. They had a strong sense of local community and adhered to prevailing moral codes of conduct dictated by the climate of the times. Puritan society also encouraged "traditional" family values whereby men and women married—and stayed married "'til death do us part"—and raised a family together. Although it is highly probable that some people have cheated on their lovers throughout history, such indiscretions were generally kept a secret so as to avoid public humiliation. This was especially the case during the Puritan days of the seventeenth century described by Nathaniel Hawthorne in *The Scarlet Letter* (1850) where an "adulteress," Hester Prynne, is publicly shamed and forced to wear a patch of fabric in the shape of an "A," signifying that she was an "adulterer." The scarlet letter indicates that she has sinned and her punishment includes public ridicule and scorn as a sinner.

The designation of certain behaviors and attitudes as "sins" has long been a ploy utilized by a community in an attempt to encourage conforming behavior among group members. We have all heard of the "Seven Deadly Sins:" pride (excessive belief in one's own abilities while ignoring the role of God); envy (desiring the traits, status, abilities, or situations of others); gluttony (the unnatural desire to consume more than one requires); lust (craving for the pleasures of the body); anger (manifested by an individual who spurns love and opts instead for fury); greed (the desire for material wealth or gain, while downplaying the spiritual realm); and sloth (the avoidance of physical or spiritual work). Throughout much of history, people have been shamed by religious others after they committed one of these "deadly sins."

A lot has changed in the United States over the centuries. Issues such as adultery and cheating are usually private concerns between the individuals involved (unless of course these people are famous). The family structure has changed dramatically and people seem less concerned about potential public ridicule. Consider that today young women willingly "Go Wild" during Spring Break; contestants with no singing ability try out for *American Idol* and throw a temper tantrum in front of TV cameras to protest their outrage over being snubbed by the judges; athletes perform "happy dances" after every minor achievement on the playing field; "shock jocks" use vulgar terms repeatedly in an attempt to draw high ratings from listeners; high school and college students get drunk and post embarrassing photos of their friends and themselves online; and people cheat on their lovers with little or no shame. In short, many people violate one, or more, of the seven deadly sins with impunity.

What accounts for such dramatic changes in attitudes regarding shameful behaviors today than compared to the past? The simple answer is: culture. The mindset of contemporary people is much different from that of previous generations and the changes in culture reflect changing attitudes toward "shameful" behaviors.

Culture

Culture, the prevailing social determinant of human behavior, reflects the norms, values and sentiments of a given society, in a given period of time. In this regard, culture can be viewed as a script for acceptable behavior among contemporary people. The prevailing culture of a society, then, dictates what behaviors are "right" and which ones are "wrong." People who violate cultural norms are generally punished, or shamed, by the greater community in one form or another. The Puritans, for example, took extreme measures to shame those who violated cultural norms related to adultery. Returning to Hawthorne's adulterous heroine of *The Scarlet Letter*, we learn that Hester Prynne is a "victim" of the cultural expectations of her society. She has been sent ahead to America by her husband, Roger Chillingworth, who must finish some business before he is able to join her. While in the New World, Prynne awaits the arrival of her husband. Instead of remaining faithful, Prynne has an affair with a Puritan minister named Arthur Dimmesdale, and gives birth to their baby, Pearl. Although Dimmesdale is guilty of having an affair with a married woman, it is Prynne alone who must face the brunt of communal punishment for adulteress behavior. She must bear the scarlet letter "A" for adultery and endure years of shame and embarrassment. Imagine if every person who has ever cheated on their spouse, or significant other, was forced to wear the scarlet letter! Why there would be people sporting "A's" everywhere.

The Puritan ethic dominated colonial America culture. It was a religious-based culture. The Judeo-Christian influence would continue to have a strong influence in the United States throughout most of its history. Religious-based cultures tend to emphasize the nonmaterial aspects of culture. Nonmaterial culture includes the more abstract creations of society, such as beliefs, values, ideology, norms, and "suitable" attitudes toward such topics as morality, sexuality, and raising a family.

A second component of culture is material culture. Material culture refers to the physical, tangible creations of a society such as automobiles, clothing, factories, sports stadiums, and computers. Although humans have always craved material goods, most people throughout history were happy, or deemed successful, if they met their basic subsistence needs of food, clothing, and shelter. This attitude would change with the rise of industrialization.

Industrialization: The Rise of Shameful Consumption and Leisure

The Industrial Revolution, which began in the late eighteenth century in England and later spread through many Western societies, including the United States, was not a single event but, rather, a number of interrelated developments that culminated in the transformation of the Western world from a largely agricultural to an overwhelmingly industrial system. Industrialization involved the substitution of machines for the muscles of animals and humans. This transformation resulted in a dramatic increase in productivity and an increased demand for more machines, more raw materials, improved means of transportation, better communication, better-educated workers, and a more specialized division of labor (Delaney, 2004).

The technological advancements brought forth by industrialization had a profound effect on the personal lives of a large segment of the population, as a growing number of people were afforded opportunities for leisure. Sociologists and economists generally regard leisure as unobligated time that is free of work or maintenance responsibilities. The term "leisure" suggests fun, distraction, and pleasure. Historically, most people had little time to pursue leisure as they were too busy trying to meet their primary needs (food, clothing, and shelter). Leisure had been reserved for the upper class; the privileged members of society. All this would change with the rise of industrialization and the resulting formation of a middle class.

Among the most notable social thinkers to examine the relationship between industrialization and the rise of the leisure class was Thorstein Veblen (1857 – 1929). Veblen was critical of the leisure class that had emerged during industrialization because people engaged in non-productive economic behavior. Veblen's definition of leisure as the non-productive consumption of time reflects his attitude that people who engage in leisure pursuits were guilty of participating in wasteful consumption. According to Veblen (1934), leisure time is consumed non-productively; first, from a sense of the unworthiness of productive work and second, as evidence of the pecuniary ability to afford a life of idleness. Veblen argued that individuals are driven to "wasteful" behaviors in an attempt to gain some level of self-esteem. Furthermore, in order to gain or hold esteem, merely possessing wealth or power is not enough. Veblen argues that wealth or power must be put into evidence for esteem to be awarded. Veblen (1947) states:

Not only does the evidence of wealth serve to impress one's importance on others and to keep their sense of his importance alive and alert, but it is of scarcely less use in building up and preserving one's self-complacency. In all but the lowest stages of culture the normally constituted man is comforted and upheld in his self-respect by 'decent surroundings' and the exemption from 'menial offices' (p. 230).

In other words, Veblen recognizes why persons participate in leisure activities, but he is also critical of such participation because he believes that leading a good productive life should be enough for one's positive self-esteem.

At the heart of Veblen's leisure theory are two concepts, *conspicuous consumption* and *conspicuous leisure*. Conspicuous consumption refers to purchasing items beyond the subsistence level. Once again, Veblen makes a connection to self-esteem as he argues that once people acquire an economic surplus they do not purchase necessity items but, instead, in an attempt to build their self-esteem, they purchase products that convey to others their increased socio-economic position. Veblen (1934) argues that once people attain a surplus they do not seek to expand their own lives more wisely, intelligently, and understandingly, but rather, they seek to impress other people with the fact that they have a surplus. Conspicuous consumption, then, involves spending money, time, and effort quite uselessly in the pleasurable business of inflating the ego. Sport sociologists Howard Nixon and James Frey (1996) further explain that conspicuous consumption amounts to "a public display of material goods, lifestyles, and behavior in a way that ostentatiously conveys privileged status to others for the purpose of gaining their approval or envy" (p.211).

Closely associated with the idea of conspicuous consumption is conspicuous leisure. Veblen describes conspicuous leisure as living a lifestyle where the pursuit of leisure and the appearance of privilege are used in order to gain approval or envy. This is also a self-esteem enhancement technique. Those who engage in conspicuous leisure are attempting to present evidence, in a public forum, of their ability to survive without having to work (or without having to work on a daily basis). In brief, conspicuous consumption and conspicuous leisure are behaviors designed to draw attention to individuals—they are, therefore, shameless. (Although, Veblen is suggesting that such people should be ashamed of their conspicuous behaviors.)

As we shall see throughout the remainder of this book, self-esteem is an important issue related to shameless behaviors. Masking shameless behaviors via conspicuous consumption and conspicuous leisure is indeed a self-esteem technique utilized by many contemporary people who historically would have been labeled quite negatively, or shamefully.

The 1960s: The Erosion of Traditional Social Norms

Industrialization ushered great socio-economic changes in Western cultures. As an increasing number of people participated in such behaviors as conspicuous consumption and conspicuous leisure, cultural norms were slowly adjusted to meet the new standards of acceptability in society. Owning a car and taking a family vacation became the norm, replacing the old norms of continuously working and acting frugally. And such is the nature of social norms; they represent established expectations of behavior that become amendable when a sizeable number of people within that culture deem new behaviors as appropriate.

Social norms are a part of the non-material culture of any given society. Norms are rules that govern behavior; they are shared expectations of what constitutes proper behavior. Once norms are established they are difficult—but not impossible—to change. Norms, like culture itself, are difficult to change because most people fear change and hold on to ideals of the past. In other words, people are creatures of habit. However, when certain behaviors become so increasingly common as to make prior norms archaic, change is inevitable.

There are two types of norms, formal and informal. Formal norms, also known as laws, are the most difficult to change. Laws are norms that have been written down by a political authority that possess designated punishments for their violation that officials have the power to enforce. It takes legal means to change a law, not simply a popular movement or collective participation. Folkways and mores represent informal norms. In contrast to laws, these norms are not written by political authorities; but they are generally understood by the members of society. Folkways are the conventional rules of everyday life that people follow almost automatically (i.e., holding the door open for the next person, turning cell phones off in public places, and similar mannerisms). These norms are relatively minor and are enforced with such informal sanctions as mild joking or ridicule when they are violated. Mores are informal but more serious norms that comprise basic moral judgments of a society. They refer to acceptable forms of behavior. Violators may face sanctions slightly more severe than those for folkways.

Despite the threat of legal punishment and public scorn, many people choose to ignore the norms of society; that is, cell phones do go off in public places and many people do not follow basic mannerisms such as holding a door open for the next person. People evade the norms of society for a variety of reasons, including the realization that certain norms are weakly enforced. For example, it is illegal for persons under the age of twenty-one to buy or drink alcoholic beverages and yet drinking by minors is commonplace. On some occasions, people may violate one norm because it is in conflict with another. For example, if a traffic officer waves a motorist through a red light (because he is part of an accident investigation team at an intersection) she is obligated to follow the instructions given by that officer and ignore the letter of the law of stopping at a red light. In other cases, however, people violate social norms simply because they disagree with them. For example, marijuana smokers smoke because they enjoy it and find the laws outlawing it archaic or meaningless.

Although the general public will always be most concerned about people who violate laws (especially crimes that cause personal harm and/or lost of property), an increasing amount of attention has been placed on those who violate informal norms. In fact, there is a general feeling among many in society that basic rules of etiquette, decorum, and proper behavior are disappearing from American culture. The argument presented here centers on the idea that there is a digression away from traditional norms and toward a blasé attitude in regards to behaviors formerly described as shameful. In other words, people today are not experiencing shame for behaviors previously described as shameful.

It is argued that this shameless attitude began in earnest in the 1960s. The decade prior (the 1950s), as characterized by the popular 1970s TV show Happy Days, is generally described in history books as a peaceful, tranquil period in American history. The 1950s, after all, followed the turbulent 1940s marked by the Second World War. The prevailing attitude of the 1950s was based on the idea that the Second World War was the war "to end all wars." Popular TV shows of the 1950s, such as I Love Lucy, stressed social conformity and clean-cut images of the American family. Lucy and Ricky, like other married TV couples, slept in separate beds—apparently creating a more wholesome, albeit less realistic, view of the American family.

The growth of the suburbs, sparked by G.I. Loans, and the corresponding "Baby Boom" were all important ingredients in the "happy days" attitude of the 1950s. However, lying just below the tranquil surface of American culture was a growing discontent. Minorities, especially African-Americans, were growing increasingly restless with their unequal status in society. The children of the 1950s became the rebel teenagers of the 1960s. Many of these rebel teenagers became hippies and openly experimented with a variety of illegal drugs. Other teenagers turned to gangs, and the gangs of the 1960s were much more violent than those of previous generations. An unpopular war in Southeast Asia fueled anti-war protests on American college campuses throughout the 1960s (and into the early 1970s). Many young males burned their draft cards and risked imprisonment for defying draft orders. Some fled to Canada to avoid serving their nation. A number of people lost trust in their government after the Vietnam War and the assassinations of President John F. Kennedy, Robert Kennedy, and Martin Luther King, Jr. A sexual revolution was ushered in with the introduction of birth control pills. Before birth control pills were available the fear of an unwanted pregnancy curtailed a great deal of premarital sex. Feminism came to the forefront in this wild decade as well. Feminists demanded women's equality and also challenged the prevailing social norms predominated by a patriarchal society. And while some feminists burned their bras, mainstream American gasped in shock disbelief.

Thus, the 1960s was a decade that witnessed a widespread challenge to traditional norms of decency and proper behavior. Many of the activities shamelessly engaged in by a variety of people in the 1960s were once considered highly shameful. But that was the point of the 1960s, to shock the traditional culture. Hippies, feminists, gang bangers, anti-war protestors, participants in premarital sex, and draft dodgers alike, did not experience a sense of shame for their behaviors.

Jeanne Hamilton, who catalogs thousands of shamelessly tacky tales of human rudeness and violations of proper etiquette on her website (www.etiquettehell.com), agrees that the 1960s was the turning point in America's traditional, cultural standards of morality. Hamilton states, "Etiquette really got thrown out during the anti-establishment, anti-authority '60s and '70s"

(Johnson, 2007: I-2). Hamilton's website is filled with a wide variety of examples of shameless behavior.

The 1960s gave way to the "Sex, Drugs, and Rock and Roll" attitude of the 1970s. Proponents of this lifestyle were also shame-free. They played rock music loudly—often to the chagrin of neighbors—freely engaged in pre-marital sex and consumed recreational drugs in the same manner that previous generations consumed the drugs of alcohol and nicotine. The 1970s accelerated the sexual revolution that had begun a decade earlier. Divorce and living together outside of marriage became increasing popular. The 1970s also played witness to legalized abortion and pills replacing the "rhythm" method as a means of birth control. Homosexuality was slowly growing in public acceptance. Hippies and recreational drug users embraced the previously shameful term of "freaks" as demonstrated by the popular comic book, The Fabulous Furry Freak Brothers. Interestingly, Eddie Vedder, lead singer of the hugely popular rock band Pearl Jam, still affectionately refers to his band's fans as "freaks."

The 1980s brought us the iconic Madonna; a performer who raised the bar on shamelessness with "S&M" inspired costumes and, later, by publishing a pornographic book. Madonna famously stated in 1983 that, "I have no shame." The 1990s brought us rap music and shock jocks who pushed the envelope on such issues as freedom of speech and expression. The 2000s have played witness to an increasing number of shameless behaviors, including an avoidance to abide by ideals of everyday etiquette (e.g., many people shamefully throw trash such as cigarettes and fast-food wrappers out of their car windows); technologically-driven drunk shamings (to be discussed in chapter 5); and MySpace and Facebook profiles that expose personal details of people's lives that previously were kept private (to be discussed in chapter 4).

According to Jean Twenge, author of *Generation Me* (2006), young people today (she uses the term "GenMe" to describe the young generation of the 2000s) are less concerned about social approval and society's standards than their peers of generations past. For example, Twenge notes that in the late 1950s, only thirty percent of young people approved of sex before marriage; now seventy-five percent approve. The disparity is even sharper for women: just 12 percent approved of premarital sex in the 1950s, compared to eighty percent today. Citing Twenge's research, Sharon Jayson (2006) states, "Among kids today, 62% of college students say they pay little attention to social conventions. In 1958, an average of 50% did. Among ages 9-12, the difference was even greater: 76% in 1999, compared with an average of 50% in 1963" (p.4D).

Twenge believes that young people don't care as much about making a good impression or displaying courtesy as their parents and grandparents did when they were growing up. Among the mannerisms ignored today is the requirement to always say "thank you" and "please" and holding a door open for the person walking behind you. In a 2002 study conducted by the non-profit research group Public Agenda; only nine percent of adults believe that kids today treat adults with respect in public.

Twenge indicates that many GenMe'ers are destined to be disillusioned, as some of their attitudes about life expectations are contradictory. For example, seventy-five percent of 2003 freshmen named "raising a family" as an important life goal, compared to just fifty-nine percent of the "Baby Boomer" generation college students in 1977. However, only 1 in 1,000 incoming 2003 college students chose "full-time homemaker" as their probable career. Due to the high cost of living, especially child care, many GenMe'ers, "mostly women, will find themselves staying at home when they never expected to do so" (Twenge, 2006:215). Nonetheless, Twenge argues that the GenMe ideology has created a profound shift in the American character, as GenMe'ers do not feel the need to gain the approval of others and do not care as much about the opinions of others on their behavioral choices compared to past generations.

Besides a change in attitude, young people today are far more distracted from day-to-day etiquette formalities than previous generations at the same age. This is due, in part, to technological advancements such as cell phones. Nearly all high school and college-aged students have cell phones and they can be seen talking or text-messaging on them continuously. People who talk on cell phones as they go from one location to the next are often distracted from such basic mannerisms as holding doors open for others and acknowledging people with whom they are in close physical proximity. Ignoring those around you is rude, but for those too busy on their cell phones, the issue of rudeness is of little, or no, consequence. After all, ignoring the person you are talking to on the phone would also be rude.

Embarrassment and Shame

Every society has cultural norms. Society expects people to willingly conform to these expectations of behavior. Laws, the most serious social norms, are enforced by agents of the judicial system (e.g., the police, prosecutors, criminal court, corrections). Enforcing mores and folkways is a little more challenging in that violating an informal norm does not lead to criminal prosecution. For example, a person who picks his nose in public is guilty of violating basic norms of etiquette, but he is not guilty of committing a crime. Because the police do not arrest people for violating folkways, it is up to members of the general public to "punish" inappropriate behaviors. As stated earlier, violations of informal norms are enforced in such mundane manners as mild joking or ridicule. At the very least, "punishment" may involve pointing out the transgression; for example, giving someone "the stare" or clearing one's throat with a "harrumph" to draw attention to patrons who are talking during a movie at the theatre. Embarrassment and shame have traditionally been used as tactics to motivate people to conform to cultural norms, especially informal norms.

It is my contention that we are entering an era where the culture of shamelessness is beginning to dominate American society. However, this is by no means intended to imply that people do not experience situations where they are embarrassed. Rather, people are less likely to experience shame today for the same behavior that would have been deemed shameful in the past. The distinction between the terms "embarrassment" and "shame" seems to underscore the culture of shamelessness. That is, people are capable of being embarrassed, but that does not mean they experience shame. A closer examination of these two often overlapping terms will be helpful, and hopefully insightful.

Embarrassment

Have you ever felt embarrassed? I would suspect we have all experienced moments of embarrassment at one point or another. I can remember when I was a senior in high school and as president of the student government it was my job to introduce the guest speaker at school general assemblies. On one particular occasion, I completely forgot the name of the speaker. I stood on stage frozen like a deer caught in headlights. I looked into the student audience for help. But they did not know the speaker's name either. And, as the rules of enforcing informal norms predicate, I was the recipient of mild ridicule. To this day, I forget many people's names. I blame it on this traumatic event from my past!

Gift-giving is a custom and social obligation found in nearly every society. Anthropologists and social exchange theorists argue that exchanging gifts binds members of society together. Exchanging gifts creates mutual obligations and increases social cohesion. However, as Thomas Hines (2002) explains in his book, *I Want That*, gift-giving also creates situations that may lead to embarrassment. For example, it is necessary to actually know something about the person you are buying a gift for, and if you don't, you realize how out of touch you are with people. Hines (2002) argues that having to buy gifts reminds us, for example, how old our nieces are, and forces us to know something about what girls their age like nowadays and to decide whether you're willing to buy it for them. Shopping makes us think about people to whom we were once close and with whom we want to maintain a connection. Hines also points out another important aspect of gift-giving in the era of shamelessness. That is, when we seek help from a sales clerk, the clerk's usual first response is, "How much do you want to spend?" Not only has the gift-giving obligation been shamelessly tied to an economic value, the relationship has also been assigned a value. Further, it forces the gift-buyer to guess what value the gift-recipient has placed on the relationship. Hines (2002) explains, "It can be very embarrassing if the person for whom you have bought a gift turns out to have spent either much more or much less on you (p. 170)."

As we all realize trying to pick out an appropriate gift is sometimes difficult. The topic of gift-giving is regularly discussed in various episodes of Seinfeld. For example, in the episode "The Deal" (#14), Jerry and Elaine have rekindled their love relationship and are dating each other once again. As I describe in my book *Seinology*, (2006) Elaine's birthday is drawing near, so Jerry discusses with George the appropriate gift to give her. Jerry wants the gift to be appropriate. But what is the appropriate gift in this case? Shamelessly, Jerry gives Elaine a card with $182 in it! Elaine is very upset. Kramer, Jerry's next door neighbor and close friend, shames Jerry by proclaiming that cash is a gift that an uncle gives a niece or nephew. Jerry becomes embarrassed by his inappropriate gift.

Embarrassing situations are certainly not limited to the social practice of gift-giving. Consider some of the following examples:

- While singing in front of a nationally televised, jammed-packed football stadium, the singer forgets the words to the national anthem.
- A cell phone goes off during class and it's the professor's phone! To make matters worse, the professor has just warned students to keep their cell phones off during class.
- While on a first date at a restaurant you suddenly realize that you forgot your wallet and have no means of paying for the bill.
- Imagine being an adult and losing to a kid on the TV show, "Are you Smarter than a 5th Grader?"
- A "best man" loses the wedding rings during the marriage ceremony.
- Realizing that your zipper is down while in public.
- Discovering that you had a piece of food stuck in between your teeth after you leave a job interview or after you asked someone out on a first date.
- Performing poorly during a public speaking engagement or having the podium you are leaning against fall apart, sending you crashing to the floor.
- Being yelled at by your boss for being incompetent while your significant other is standing nearby.
- Calling someone by the wrong name while on a date; or worse, during a moment of intimacy.
- Having a visible urine stain (or water stain from the sink splashing that looks like a urine stain) on your pants.
- A student who falls asleep in class not only looks like a fool for such humiliating self-shaming behavior; it can be compounded if he or she begins to snore. A student also experiences embarrassment if he or she has not completed the assigned reading and therefore cannot contribute to class discussion.
- Someone who pees their pants for any reason, but especially because of drunkenness.
- Parents who cannot control their unruly children in public; especially in grocery or shopping stores.
- Parking your car on a steep hill and failing to turn your wheels to rub against the curb and/or forgetting to engage the emergency parking brake only to find the car crashed at the bottom of the hill the next morning.
- A waiter or waitress trips and falls and spills multiple plates of food and glasses of beverages.

These are just a few examples of embarrassing situations that people may find themselves in. In each of these cases, the participant has failed in a central aspect of his or her role performance. People become uncomfortable and experience anxiety (embarrassment) when they realize that they failed in their role presentation. This awareness triggers psychological, sociological, and physiological reactions. Psychologically, embarrassed people have their self-esteem and self-identities compromised. Sociologically, embarrassed persons will experience social anxiety and may fear future public engagements. Physiologically, embarrassed people may blush, stutter, sweat, experience an increased heart rate, and fumble about.

A further elaboration of embarrassment reveals its proximity to shame. Embarrassment "reflects a failure to present oneself in the way one would have wished" (Edelmann, 1987:14). Embarrassment is usually regarded as a form of social anxiety closely related to shyness, audience anxiety and shame (Buss, 1980; Schlenker and Leary, 1982; Edelmann, 1987). The fear of embarrassment plays a central role in the experience of social anxiety. Social anxiety often becomes termed "embarrassment" or "shame" depending upon the nature of the event (Edelmann, 1987). When someone is embarrassed or shamed a discrepancy between one's current unintended self presentation and one's desired self presentation occurs (Asendorpf, 1984). Goffman (1956) points out that we are capable of recognizing extreme embarrassment in others, as well as ourselves, by objective signs of emotional disturbance: blushing, fumbling, mumbling, stuttering, an unusually low- or high-pitched voice, quavering speech or breaking of the voice, sweating, tremor of the hand, and absent-mindedness.

Embarrassing situations usually involve people who have violated minor social norms; they have committed a faux pas (a slip or blunder in etiquette, manners, or conduct; an embarrassing social blunder or indiscretion), or an impropriety. Thus, while it is understandable why the embarrassed person may experience anxiety, she should not necessarily feel ashamed for her behaviors. After all, accidents and minor transgressions will occur, and we have all experienced embarrassing moments in our lives. As a result, it is not necessary to experience shame over embarrassing situations. Shame, then, is a stronger emotion than embarrassment.

Shame

Shame involves intense negative emotion having to do with the self in relation to standards and responsibilities (Lewis, 1998). Buss (1980) argues that shame is a more severe feeling because it has "moral implications;" whereas embarrassment does not. For example, someone who slips and falls in a mud puddle in front of others will experience embarrassment, but not shame. Falling in mud is embarrassing but it is hardly a behavior that one needs to feel ashamed of committing. A traitor will experience shame (when caught) because of the built-in moral implication of betraying one's country. The traitor should feel ashamed because he has brought dishonor and disgrace upon himself. Conditions of disgrace and dishonor are beyond that of simple embarrassment; they involve guilt.

Guilt, then, is a component of shame. Guilt involves feelings of remorse and regret for one's actions and shame refers to the feelings that one has about the guilt for violating a social norm. Joyce Brothers (2005) explains, "While guilt is the feeling that you have done something wrong, shame is the feeling that there's something wrong about you. Nothing could be more all-encompassing. When we've had too much exposure to shame, our joy in life is severely diminished. That's why the self-esteem movement declared war on shame decades ago" (p.5). Guilt is something that develops from one's conscience and is typically expressed by such sentiments as, "I did something bad" or "I did something wrong."

Embarrassment, on the other hand, does not have the component of guilt. To contrast embarrassment and shame imagine a series of provocative photos of a young woman suddenly appearing on the Internet while she has been thrust in the public eye (for example, as a contestant on *American Idol*). Let's say these photos were taken while this woman was on a vacation with a group of friends. These photos were meant for private consumption. And while the content of the photos may be embarrassing if certain people view them (such as the young woman's family), the people involved have nothing to be ashamed of because the photos were never intended for public viewership. The person who leaked these photos, however, has committed a violation worthy of shame because he or she is guilty of violating codes of honor between friends.

It also important to point out that the designation of certain norm violations as shameful involves a judgment from others. And therein lies the peculiar nature of culture. Members of a particular society dictate the cultural norms that others are expected to abide by. Inevitably, there will be those who disagree with certain communal expectations of their behaviors. In this regard, whether someone experiences shame or not will be determined, at least in part, by perception. That is, if certain behaviors are not perceived as shameful, how can someone experience shame? Furthermore, if no one experiences shame, how can social norms exist? The culture of shamelessness presents many intriguing questions.

The Culture of Shamelessness Is Not Unchallenged

Throughout this book, evidence of the growing culture of shamelessness will be presented. However, it is also argued that as the culture of shamelessness expands the number of shamings also increases. Shamings may be either formal or informal. Chapter 2 explores formal shamings, such as military court martials, judicial punishments, and workplace mobbings. Formal shamings are accompanied by degradation ceremonies. Degradation ceremonies are conducted by formal organizations and are designed to compromise the offender's self-esteem and identity by stigmatizing, embarrassing, and shaming individuals. Informal shamings are discussed in chapter 3. Informal shamings are quasi-degradation ceremonies in that the perpetrators of these shamings are not formal organizations but, instead, regular people (e.g., friends, family members, sports teammates). This chapter also explores the idea that people actually find joy in shaming others for their shameful transgressions. Finding joy in other people's follies is an important aspect of the growing culture of shamelessness. However, the large number of informal shamings would suggest that the culture of shamelessness is meeting resistance.

Chapter 2

Formal Shamings:
Degradation Ceremonies Designed to
Compromise Self-esteem and Identity

"There are two ways to get rid of thorns and wicket persons; using footwear in the first case and in the second shaming them so that they cannot raise their faces again, thus keeping them at a distance"— Chanakya (Indian politician, strategist, and writer, 350 BC – 275 BC)

Military personnel generally possess a positive sense of self and a favorable identity. In an attempt to elevate his own sense of self, a Montana man, William C. Horvath, lied to his probation officer about having served in the military. Horvath knew that if his lie was revealed that he risked punishment; this is true any time someone violates a social norm. Horvath's lie, and criminal offense (making false statements), was discovered and U.S. District Judge Donald Molloy punished him with four months of house arrest and four years of probation. A seemingly reasonable punishment. However, the judge did not stop there. Molloy felt that Horvath's behavioral indiscretion deserved an additional punishment, a formal judicial public shaming. Judge Molloy tacked on an additional punishment by sentencing Horvath to wear a sandwich board that read, "I am a liar, I am not a Marine." Horvath was sentenced to wear the shaming board for a total of 50 hours outside the Missoula courthouse. The judge also ordered Horvath to write letters of apology to the U.S. Marine Corps and the Veterans of Foreign Wars (*Los Angeles Times*, 7/8/6:A19).

Horvath was the recipient of a formal (judicial) public shaming. Public shamings as a form of criminal punishment have been a part of human history in most cultures throughout recorded time. Many formal shamings come in the form of degradation ceremonies.

In this chapter, we shall explore how formal shamings, such as degradation ceremonies, are utilized in an attempt to compromise one's identity, self-esteem, and presentation of self.

The Purpose of Formal Shamings

The purpose of any formal shaming is to make the offender feel extreme guilt for violating a law. In other words, punishment is not enough. The offense is considered so distasteful that the whole community should be made aware of it. Communal involvement reaffirms what French sociologist Emile Durkheim labeled the "collective conscience." Durkheim (1933) defines the collective conscience as "The totality of beliefs and sentiments common to average citizens of the same society" (p. 79). Durkheim believed that public ceremonies of punishments help to strengthen communal bonds. However, Durkheim also argued that public shamings are more characteristic of primitive societies than they are of modern societies. And, for the most part, citizens of modern societies frown upon the idea of extreme public shamings—such as executions—but have a growing acceptance toward more mild forms of public shamings. Furthermore, there is a growing popular collective conscience that seems to endorse the idea of public executions; perhaps on a pay-per-view form of broadcast. Imagine the spectacle of people gathering at bars and cheering an execution as it occurs live on television.

Formal shamings, then, provide two primary purposes. First, they represent attempts—by those who wish to hold onto traditional cultural ideals—to enforce long-held beliefs on core values. When punishments are made public, the alarm has been sounded to the greater community to pay attention to what happens when someone violates cultural laws. The second purpose of a formal shaming is to send a strong message to the violator. Punishments that are made public are designed to shame the violator to the point where his or her very sense of self is destroyed, or at the very least, greatly modified. Thus, when someone has been formally shamed, his or her very presentation of self has been altered.

Identity and the Presentation of Self

Generally, individuals are very concerned with their sense of identity and presentation of self. We attempt to manage and control our sense of identity when we present ourselves to others. "The way we are treated by others typically depends on what those others think of us, and because of this, whether or not we are consciously aware of it, we often try to influence the impressions of us that others form" (Miller, 1996:110). The process of trying to control how we are viewed by others is called "self presentation" or "impression management" (Leary and Kowalski, 1990). Furthermore, as Schlenker (1980) states, impression management is "a central part of the very nature of social interaction" (p.7). Erving Goffman also argued that impression management was an important device utilized by individuals in their presentation of self. Goffman utilized a dramaturgical perspective and compares all human interaction to a theatrical or dramatic performance. Society is viewed as a stage where humans are actors giving performances for audiences. "While acting, individuals attempt to present themselves according to their identity constructs. The 'self label' is an identity that one presents to others in an attempt to manage their impression of him or her. Individuals deliberately give off signs to provide others with information about how to 'see' them" (Delaney, 2005:122).

Because of the importance placed on self presentation, most people attempt to avoid embarrassing situations that may lead to private and/or public shame. Degradation ceremonies are an example of an effort to embarrass specific people because of their behavior. Individuals generally attempt to avoid being victimized by a degradation ceremony because it may negatively affect their self-presentation, identity and self-esteem, and their future career possibilities.

Oddly, some people will place themselves in a situation where ceremonies of degradation are almost surely to follow. This is particularly true for some young adults, especially college students who risk being shamed as a result of their drunken behavior. Most college students drink; some drink a great deal and may find themselves the "victim" of a "drunk shaming." (Note: Drunk shamings will be discussed in detail in chapter 5.) Degradation ceremonies are performed to alert a larger audience that an individual(s) has violated social norms. Generally, people who are publicly shamed feel remorse and suffer a blow to their self-esteem. As a result, they experience a negative transformation in their sense of self and identity.

Sense of Identity

A sense of identity is a necessary element in the development of self and self-esteem. Identity is comprised of the defining characteristics of an individual that are unique to that person, and help distinguish him or her from others (Ruyter and Conroy, 2002). As Schlenker (1980) suggests, all aspects of our appearance (including how we dress, body size and shape, hair color, etc.); background (e.g., home environment); intelligence; and general behavior (degree of anxiety) serve as factors that shape one's identity. Personal identity is linked to an individual's goals and aspirations. Without a sense of identity and life goals, individuals wander about aimlessly. "One's identity then is a composite of all aspects of an individual which go towards creating our own view of ourselves as well as how we are viewed by an audience" (Edelmann, 1987:20). Possessing a sense of identity helps to provide individuals with a certain level of stability and predictability in their social worlds. A sense of identity is a necessary element in the development of self and self-concept. As defined by Cobb (2001), "self-concept is a way of explaining and interpreting the facts one experiences in daily life, a way of constructing the self" (p.211). It also allows us to maintain a sense of order and continuity (like a script or guide) that will remain consistent over time, giving us a baseline in which we can merge new information.

One's identity is shaped by both personal and group needs. Identity theory, which is based on this principle, argues that individuals attempt to establish and maintain their self-concepts for both themselves and others (Gecas and Burke, 1995). People develop an individual identity because of their need to define themselves in their own context (Phinney, 2000). This is accomplished through the identification and definition of ideals. From these ideals individuals set goals and seek out resources that will increase the likelihood that they will come to fruition. Various factors influence one's ability and/or motivation to reach these goals. They include past experiences of success and failure, a positive support system, access to resources, and positive role models. Established individual identities are maintained through social interactions with others (Stryker and Serpe, 1994). "As people monitor other people's reactions to them, they have feelings about these reactions and respond to these reflected appraisals in the process of building their own sense of self" (Jaret, Reitzes, and Shapkina, 2005:403).

Individuals also develop a sense of self based on their group identities. Humans are social creatures and generally enjoy the company of significant others—people who share similar ideals, hopes, dreams, desires and general outlooks on life. Individuals seek a sense of unity and purpose with others. The group identity fulfills this need (Shu-fang Dien, 2000). A group identity is developed through interactions with others. Bits and pieces of information are taken from every person and social situation. A group identity is generally formed at the time of birth when the child becomes a member of a family. New group identities emerge when the child forms play groups with neighborhood kids and schoolmates. Often, during adolescence, new cliques and peer groups are formed. Children grow older and attempt to establish an identity separate from the family, but lacking complete confidence to strike out on their own, they find comfort in joining a peer group with like-minded people. Group membership increases one's sense of security and support. College students, like many young adults, experience great pressure to try and fit into a group. Drinking alcohol often serves as a buffer and becomes an accepted form of behavior among college students. Many feel pressure to drink heavily and boast about their drunken exploits. When friends participate with each other in drunken exploits they are helping to solidify their group membership (albeit not in the healthiest manner).

There are times when individuals have a group identity thrust upon them. This results in a compromised individual identity. In many cases, the group identity is forged by having the individuals within the group wear the same uniform. Prison inmates must all wear the same uniform. Athletes in team sports wear the same uniform, as do school children at private schools, and many work environments require that employees all wear the same uniform. Although athletes on team sports seldom, if ever, express concern over wearing the same outfits as others, many school children fret that wearing standardized uniforms stifles their self-expression. This concern had far greater merit in the past than it does today. As a person who was forced to go to a private school and wear a school uniform (green pants, white shirt and tie), I can attest first hand how monotonous it was to have to wear the same style of clothing every day. From the time I finished my secondary private school education to this day, I refuse to wear a dress (collar) white shirt! Today's school uniforms, however, offer a little more flexibility and individual self-expression. Still, there are many pros and cons regarding school uniforms.

Among the people who promote school uniforms are school administrators, some parents, a small percentage of students, and a wide variety of education experts. The school uniform itself is generally more casual than when I was a school-aged child. Instead of the traditional formal pants, white shirt and tie for boys and jumpers and white shirts for girls, most school uniforms today include khakis or jeans and knit shirts of varying colors. Establishing a school uniform that allows for options is an important step in allowing school children the opportunity to maintain an individual sense of identity.

People who promote school uniforms have their reasons and now that I am an adult it is easier to understand their justifications. Educators believe that students who wear school uniforms perform better academically in school. The simple fact that students do not have to focus on their wardrobe frees their minds to concentrate on more important things, like their school work. Conversely, shallow students who are consumed by what they wear are generally not as focused on what the need to learn. Thus, wearing a school uniform creates a more serious tone within the school environment. In this regard, students who wear school uniforms act more appropriately because they are focused on their studies. School uniforms, then, have the uncanny ability to instill a sense of discipline at the school. Furthermore, because students do not have to spend much time preparing their clothes in the morning, many school districts that have adopted a uniform policy also believe that school uniforms improve school attendance.

Educators also believe that school uniforms help to create a sense of community among students. Wearing school uniforms reduces the obvious socio-economic disparity among children and places everyone on an equal plane. In this regard, students from wealthy families will not be able to flaunt their advantageous social position via such examples of conspicuous consumption as designer jeans and other clothing outfits. Requiring students to wear a school uniform also helps school officials to recognize those who do not belong on campus, which in turn, may potentially reduce violence. In California, the Long Beach Unified School District adopted a mandatory uniform policy in 1994. Since then, school officials report that crime has dropped by seventy-six percent and attendance has reached an all-time high. The lower level of violence in the Long Beach schools is attributed to the wearing of school uniforms because students are not allowed to wear gang colors in school. Theft is also reduced when students wear the same uniforms. After all, if everyone is wearing the same clothing and similar shoes, the enticement to steal designer shoes and clothing is eliminated.

When students wear a school uniform, teachers and administrators are free from the cumbersome chore of policing what students wear; for example, determining whether certain T-shirts are offensive or whether girls' skirts are too short. In brief, people who promote school uniforms see numerous social and economic benefits. This does not, however, stop others from waging fierce battles to assure that school uniforms are not implemented in all schools.

Parents who support school uniforms will cite many of the previously mentioned justifications but generally emphasize their displeasure with the current style of clothing many children have adopted. These parents are relieved that they do not have to argue with their children over the appropriateness of wearing such clothing items as tank tops, blouses that expose the midriff, baggy shorts and pants, hooded sweatshirts, and so on. When school children wear a uniform, they cannot wear shameless articles of clothing. Also, parents do not have to worry about "keeping up with the Jones'" wherein kids are constantly comparing themselves to others in school. When parents are asked about the concern that their children may lose their sense of self and individuality while wearing a school uniform, many respond that children "can be individuals on the weekend!"

There are a number of reasons why people oppose school uniforms. Some families fear that requiring uniforms might interfere with their children wearing religious clothing (a topic of great debate in such countries as France and England where students are not allowed to wear religious garb). And although it is extremely difficult to argue with the validity of school uniforms eliminating gang members' opportunity to express their gang identity via clothing, there are those who question whether Long Beach school officials can attribute the drastic reduction in crime solely, or even primarily, to their school uniform policy.

Older students, especially those in junior high school and high school, have a tendency to flat-out resent school uniforms. This resentment can potentially cause a great deal of harm and counter balance all the positive reasons cited in favor of school uniforms. As any student who has ever worn a uniform can attest, there are still ways to express individualism. This is especially true for girls who may choose to express themselves through make-up, jewelry accessories, and short skirts. Boys and girls alike can express themselves by how they act, walk, wear their hair, pull their socks over their pants, and a wide variety of behaviors designed to counteract the "herd mentality" of school uniforms. In short, there are a number of ways to express oneself even when wearing a uniform. Despite this, the primary reasons cited against school uniforms still center on the belief that uniforms stifle, or even violate, students' freedom of expression. And while it is true that self-expression is an important aspect in the developmental process, as previously stated, there are a variety of means of expressing oneself within the group context.

Still, detractors of school uniforms argue that students' individual identities are not being nurtured in an environment where students are required to wear a uniform. I have often wondered if the parents, administrators, parents and educators who promote school uniforms would like to wear a uniform themselves. At Catholic schools this question is answered, in part, as priests and nuns wear uniforms. (Note: Laypersons who teach at Catholic schools do not wear a uniform.) Even so, many nuns and priests today enjoy a more relaxed uniform than those from the past, or refuse to wear the religious garb at all.

Students who wear a school uniform may feel as though their individuality has been compromised by the clothes they wear but they still possess the opportunity to express themselves in the classroom via creative thinking and class discussion. After all, the primary purpose of having students attend school is to learn, and students' identities are best illustrated by how they perform in the classroom and not how they dress.

Whereas students who wear a uniform to school still have the opportunity to express their individual identities, there are many adults who must wear uniforms and are not afforded this luxury.

The Shame of McJobs: Work That Is So Easy a Caveman Can Do It!

If wearing a uniform in school causes angst, imagine wearing a uniform as an adult! There are a variety of settings where adults are dressed alike. In prison, for example, the inmates wear one uniform and the correctional officers another uniform. It is kind of like rival sports teams or rival gang members where everyone wears a uniform so that we can easily distinguish between the "good guys" and the "bad guys." Many companies require that their personnel wear uniforms while at work. For example, delivery persons (e.g., FedEx drivers), postal carriers, retail suppliers (e.g., beer and soda delivery workers), police officers, and security guards must all wear uniforms. Nearly all these workers have compromised their individual identities in favor of the organization that has employed them. And yet, in most cases, these people must still think and be prepared to handle unexpected situations as they arise. Such is not the case for people who hold "McJobs."

What is a McJob, you may ask? McJobs is an integral aspect of George Ritzer's famous concept of "McDonaldization." According to Ritzer (1993), McDonaldization is "the process by which the principles of the fast food restaurant are coming to dominate more and more sectors of American society as well as the rest of the world" (p.91). The McDonaldization process has extended beyond the fast food industry and now extends to a variety of industries including: toy stores (such as Toys R Us), bookstores (B. Dalton's), newspapers (USA Today), child care (Kinder Care), learning (Sylvan Learning Centers), and a number of other businesses (Delaney, 2005). Ritzer uses the term "McJobs" to describe the typical job functions associated within businesses that employ the McDonaldization mentality. Beyond the fact that most of these employees wear a uniform, a McJob tends to:

> Involve a series of simple tasks in which the emphasis is on performing each as efficiently as possible. Second, the time associated with many of the tasks is carefully calculated and the emphasis on the quantity of time a task should take tends to diminish the quality of the work from the point of view of the worker. That is, tasks are so simplified and streamlined that they provide little or no meaning to the worker. Third, the work is predictable; employees do and say essentially the same things hour after hour, day after day. Fourth, many non-

human technologies are employed to control workers and reduce them to robot-like actions (Ritzer, 2002:142).

As Ritzer (2002) indicates, for many people, working at a fast-food restaurant (a McJob) is likely to be the first job someone holds. In fact, it is estimated that McDonalds is the first job for one of every 15 workers and that one in every eight Americans has worked at a McDonalds at some time in his or her life. This is the reason why Ritzer uses McDonald's as his exemplar to explain his theory of rationality. Further, whether or not a person has worked at a McDonalds specifically, chances are, many people have held a McJob at some point in their life. A large number of college students currently hold McJobs. Holding a McJobs has such a negative influence on identity; that it often reaches the point where it is nearly degrading.

Although Ritzer uses the terms "McDonaldization" and "McJobs" in a demeaning manner, he is not picking on the fast food restaurant McDonald's specifically. Rather, he uses these terms to describe the growing application rationalization principles in many jobs, especially the service industry. The McDonald's Corporation, on the other hand, is taking such terms personally and is especially upset with the definition of the term "McJob." In 2007, McDonald's revived its campaign to banish the word "McJob" from dictionaries! After an unsuccessful attempt, in 2003, to have the *Merriam-Webster* dictionary remove "McJob" from its dictionaries, McDonald's set its sights on dictionaries in the United Kingdom. The primary English dictionary, *The Oxford English Dictionary*, defines the noun as "an unstimulating, low-paid job with few prospects, especially one created by the expansion of the service sector." Walt Riker, a McDonald's spokesperson, claims that the term "McJob" is "incredibly demeaning to a terrific workforce" (*Chicago Tribune*, 3/21/07). Interestingly, Jay Leno discussed this "controversy" during his opening monologue on March 23, 2007. Questioning McDonald's claim that the term "McJob" is demeaning, Leno quipped, "And the paper hats they make their employees wear are not demeaning?!" Apparently Leno doesn't realize that the hat makes the uniform!

According to Ritzer, the McDonaldization process possesses five dominant elements: efficiency, calculability, predictability, control and replacement of people with nonhuman technologies, and the irrationality of rationality. Having discussed these principles with my students, many come away with the realization that they hold a McJob even if it is not at a fast-food restaurant. As one student stated, "I was a slave to the cash register in a red apron." This student described how all employees, except the manager, wore an oversized red apron with a plastic name tag with the company's name embroidered on the front right of chest area. "This gave creepy, crafty men an excuse to stare at our chests," she explained. Employers are often unaware, or unconcerned, with the degradation that employees experience wearing certain uniforms. The outfits worn by "Hooters" waitresses are a perfect example of a degrading uniform.

A number of other student experiences are shared here along with an elaboration of the five principles of the McDonaldization process.

1. Efficiency – This dimension refers to choosing the means to reach a specific end, rapidly, and with the least amount of cost or effort. Theoretically, this dimension of rationality is designed to benefit the customer; after all, the less time the customer has to wait for an order, the happier he or she will be. Unfortunately, in an effort to speed along the process of delivering food quickly, many restaurants provide the basics of the meal, but the customer must still take the time to go the "fixing bar" in order to add such items as onions, lettuce, ketchup, and napkins and straws. The "salad bar" is the ultimate example of an effort by the restaurant to make customers work by "serving" themselves.

Some retail stores have taken the efficiency idea to the extreme. For example, customers are now expected to "check" themselves at the cash register. They scan the product codes, bag their groceries, or other retail items, and then feed a machine their payment. At many chain theatres (e.g., Regal Cinema), patrons use computerized touch screens to purchase their tickets. Movie theatre customers who purchase concession items are also given just the basics and expected to take care of their other needs at the "fixing station." At Blockbuster Video, customers are expected to find a desired movie by themselves and without help from the employees. A student explains, "We are told to direct them [customers] in the right direction; however, we are not expected to take the person to the movie or get it for them. They are expected to do just about everything themselves...basically, they are unpaid labor that Blockbuster capitalizes on."

At the highly popular Wegmans grocery stores (found primarily in New York state), cashiers are timed on their efficiency skills. Cashiers are expected to maintain an IPM (Items per Minute) pace that exceeds sixteen. This is designed to assure that customers are getting through the lines fast enough. Only employees with high IPMs are permitted to work on the express lanes.

2. Calculability – The McDonaldization process involves an emphasis on things that can be calculated, counted, and quantified. In an effort to assure a certain quantity, quality is often compromised. Thus, customers are served with "Big Macs," "Whoppers," and "Big Gulps," but they are not promised high quality food. In fact, many foods prepared at fast food restaurants are microwaved; and microwaving food obviously detracts from its quality. According to Ritzer, the calculability element of McDonaldization leaves the employees with little or no chance of personal meaning, and therefore they are filled with feelings of alienation.

At stores like Blockbuster, or Borders, super-sizing food is not the issue but getting people checked out as soon as possible remains a standard. Further, employees try to get customers to join various promotional programs that, in the long run, will amount to increased sales for the company and unused services on the part of the customer. At many businesses, including convenience stores and movie theatres, every cup, nacho tray, etc., is counted. Thus, from the point of view of the business, customers do not really purchase a product; they are paying for the container in which it is served.

3. Predictability – Predictability involves the attempt to structure the environment in such a way that customers can assume that certain products will always be available and that the quality of those products are consistent even if not good. Further, employees are trained to behave consistently in every similar situation. In this regard, employees are not required to think, but to respond to stimuli. For example, many retail stores that sell alcohol have implemented a policy wherein employees are required to ask customers for ID, proving they are of age. Such a policy eliminates the need for an employee to "guess" whether or not the customer is of age. It also eliminates the clerk's need to use his or her brain to figure out whether someone is borderline legal age or clearly over age twenty-one. The clerk's intelligence is further insulted if she has proofed this customer before and knows that he is of age. In addition, the customer may be famous or well-known by the clerk and yet he is still required to proof the purchaser. Relying on a store policy that requires a cashier to proof all customers eliminates the need for eye contact between the two and diminishes the value of being a loyal customer to a particular store. Regular customers want to be valued and recognized. Proofing a regular customer repeatedly defies rationality and good manners. Thus, the principle of predictability is potentially embarrassing and insulting to both the employee and customer.

Fast food restaurants and retail stores thrive on predictability. In most cases, McDonald's, Wal-Mart, Borders Bookstores, Blockbuster Video Stores, Regal Theatres, and so on, are designed in eerily identical fashion from one location to the next. Customers can generally expect employees to act in the same way from one location to the next. This is because employees who hold McJobs are generally given instructional videos to watch so that they know how to respond to given situations.

Retail stores such as Wal-Mart will carry the same products, place them on the same shelves as every other store location, and these items will be labeled by overhead signs. Every Regal Theatre will have popcorn, soda, and a consistent selection of candy. Blockbuster Videos will place "New Releases" in alphabetical order along the perimeter of the store and an employee will greet customers when they enter. Further, one can predict with certainty that employees at these locations will also be wearing the same uniform.

4. Control and replacement of people with nonhuman technologies – Rationalists do not deal well with uncertainty and unplanned events. Because people often act irrationally, the McDonaldization process attempts to replace humans with nonhuman technologies wherever possible. In an effort to maintain control, the fast-food mentality is dominated by the ideal of prepackaged, premeasured products. This frees employees from the need to think; they simply need to follow instructions and push buttons. For example, checkers at supermarkets don't have to think; they simply scan the barcode on the products being purchased. The employee at the french fry station at McDonald's doesn't have to think about whether the fries are cooked, he just waits for the bell to ring. The control aspect is so dominant in many industries that airplanes nearly fly themselves with the assistance of computerized equipment. Following a dress code, pressing

buttons, and going through the motion are all characteristics of the control aspects of McJobs.

5. Irrationality of Rationality – Ritzer indicates that some companies have relied so heavily on rationality that they have forgotten about the human element of business. Employees often resemble zombies and when customers ask them unique questions they are baffled as how to answer them. Furthermore, many customers are acting irrationally. The quality of food at fast-food restaurants doesn't come near the quality of food that people could prepare for themselves. And if a customer calculates the amount of time she spends serving herself compared to the amount of time the employee spends with her, she may wonder, "Where is the service?" Gas stations were among the first industries to introduce the idea of "self serve." But "self serve" is an oxymoron. The word "service" means to serve another. How can someone possibly serve himself? In other words, there is no such thing as self-service. Customer irrationality comes in many forms; for example, a number of customers will pay double the price for such conveniences as sliced fruit at a grocery store when they could buy whole pieces of fruit and slice it themselves at home.

As the McDonaldization process indicates, a number of people are engaged in McJobs that are relatively unchallenging, and in some cases, degrading. In this regard, it could be argued that McJobs are a type of degradation ceremony in that employees' lives have become so formalized and predictable that even a caveman can perform their duties. One student describes her McJob at a chain grocery store as being so structured that she knows even if she is sick she can do her job because "of the lack of thinking that I have to do." A student who works at Blockbuster Video echoes this sentiment and proclaims that she does not "bust any brain cells" doing her job. She further states, "The entire system is designed so that the worker does not have to think. We are robots, spitting out exactly what corporate wants us to say and do it with a smile."

McJobs represent situations where a person's identity is compromised because he or she is not afforded an opportunity to express a sense of self. The McDonaldization process is an aspect of the general culture of shamelessness wherein customers are expected to "serve" themselves and employees are treated as drones. In short, McJobs are degrading because they hamper individuals' attempt to reach their full potential. The growing culture of shamelessness is exemplified by one student's reaction to his McJob: "Because I go to school full time and my life is hectic, I like being able to go to work and not have to actually think about anything. I cannot imagine having to work twice as hard…So, the customer's suffering is actually my gain." Shameful!

The Self

An important elicitor of shame is a threat to the social self (Gruenewald, et. al., 2004). A sense of self involves the process whereby individuals reflect on themselves as objects (Mead, 1934). The self is something which must develop; it is not initially there at birth, but arises through interaction with others. George

Herbert Mead believes that newborn babies do not have a sense of themselves as objects; instead they respond automatically and selfishly to hunger, discomfort, and the various stimuli around them. The development of self occurs when the young child learns to use significant symbols, especially language. It is during early childhood that individuals begin to create a model in their minds of the world around them as well as how they, as physical beings (objects), fit into the model. Essential to development, this baseline model enables individuals to compare and contrast new experiences which will help determine and shape later behavior. Young children are referred to as so-and-so's son or daughter, perhaps even introducing themselves that way. Consequently, a child's first identity is directly tied to the family. Children will also often take on the perceived attributes of another individual in the family. For example, if they see their father as smart and funny or their mother as generous and kindhearted they will try to model these admired qualities.

Defining the term "self" varies across academic disciplines (Rubinstein and de Medeiros, 2005). For our purposes, the self is viewed as a multifaceted and dynamic aspect of the human that allows for self-reflection and contemplation that is influenced by personal experiences and interactions with others. The development of self is a lifelong process and is influenced by numerous factors. Both the individual and group self are continuously being revised and adjusted, through the combination of past, present, and future experiences, in order to accommodate for change. The developmental process itself begins in early childhood. The development of self is critical for the creation of consciousness, as well as for the ability of the young child to take the role of the other and to visualize their own performances from the point of view of others (Delaney, 2004). Mead (1934), in his theory of the development of self, argued that the emergence of the social self occurs during childhood when the child must learn to understand the meanings of symbols and language. Mead believed that most learning took place through various forms of play.

Self-esteem

In general, people want others to see them as they see themselves. When this is the case individuals have formed positive self-appraisals of their identities. Self-appraisal, or self-verification, processes impact one's self-esteem (Cast and Burke, 2002). "Individuals are motivated to match their identity with situational meanings that support and enhance self-esteem. Through reflected appraisals, individuals do not neutrally assess their behaviors, but selectively emphasize outcomes that support identities and create positive self-esteem" (Jaret, et. al., 2005:405). Morris Rosenberg (1965) defines self-esteem as a positive or negative attitude toward a particular object, namely, the self. From this definition, self-esteem has two different connotations. One connotation is that of high self-esteem, where individuals think highly of themselves and feel that they have value and self-worth. On the other hand, low self-esteem leads to feelings of negative self-worth, doubt, self-rejection and self-contempt. Most researchers that incorporate tests of self-esteem include a third category—moderate self-esteem, for those who fall in between the high and low categories of self-esteem.

When I administer Rosenberg's classic self-esteem measurement test I make a point of telling students that self-esteem is dynamic—meaning, measurements of self-esteem are subject to change based on an individual's circumstances at the time of taking the test.

Self-esteem dictates how an individual views oneself as an object. Because self-esteem dictates how people view themselves, it is also associated with one's mental health and general psychological well-being. High self-esteem is associated with such things as positive ego functioning, good personal adjustment, and an internal sense of control. Conversely, low self-esteem is often connected to a number of negative attitudes, such as feelings of inadequacy, a sense of unworthiness, increased anxiety, depression, suicide, and certain mental health disorders (Mruk, 1999).

Furthermore, one's level of self-esteem often dictates, or impacts, courses of action taken by individuals. Self-esteem plays an important role in whether or not a person attempts to optimize his or her life situations. People with high self-esteem tend to be more optimistic and will seek out social and physical resources necessary to increase the likelihood that they accomplish their goals. Not surprisingly, higher levels of achievement are attained through optimization (Lerner, Freund, Stefanis, Habermas, 2001). Such things as motivation, and parental and peer support, are often linked to an adolescent's pursuit of increased resources. Often, if people have a negative attitude about themselves they will not believe that they can accomplish anything and therefore will not try.

As Crocker, Lee and Park (2004) propose, everyone is free to choose courses of actions that may increase, or decrease, individual levels of self-esteem. We are free to engage in behaviors that elevate our sense of self, just as we are free to choose behaviors that may cause harm to our self-esteem. Participating in group activities may stimulate both results. The social groups that individuals join reflect their current needs, personal identity, and sense of self. Group membership may result in either increased or decreased self-esteem as groups themselves have an identity and image throughout the greater community. If the group joined is popular, one's self-esteem is increased; however, if it is perceived as a lesser group the members may experience a "negative social identity" (Shu-fang Dien, 2000:6). Shu-fang Dien proposed that group identity is "the outcome of the interaction between the capabilities, limitations and identities of its individual members, the structure of the group including the network of social and power relationships it entails, and its position in relation to other groups" (Shu-fang Dien, 2000:5).

Presentation of Self

As demonstrated thus far, one's identity is tied to self-feelings and other people's assessments. If others do not see us as we wish, we have failed in our presentation of self. As Edelmann (1987) explains, "Self presentation refers to the attempts we make to control the self-relevant images that we project to others" (p.16). As best articulated by Erving Goffman (1959) the *presentation of self* involves the description of an individual as an active and reflective self capable of making a vast number of choices in determining how the self should be

presented in varies social situations in which one is found. Individuals deliberately give off signs to provide others with clues about how to "see" them. "Information about the individual helps to define the situation, enabling others to
know in advance what he will expect of them and what they may expect of him.
Informed in these ways, the others will know how best to act in order to call
forth a desired response from him. For those present, many sources of information become accessible and many carriers (or 'sign-vehicles') become available
for conveying this information" (Goffman, 1959:1). Individuals are constantly
striving to maintain an outward expression of their identity. They create definitions of situations that best fit their needs, will attempt to avoid blame and social
disapproval form others, self-promote, omit negative events from their past in
front of those who may "judge" them (e.g., potential employers, dating partners), and in some cases, intimidate others into accepting the preferred self.

Expanding on Goffman's ideas, there are a number of self-presentational
strategies that individuals may employ in an attempt to present a certain image.
Baum (2006) believes that people want to be liked and respected by others, especially those who are most important to their social identities and therefore
attempt to present favorable impressions to win popularity and respect. However, not all people are worried about being liked by others. In fact, they may
thrive on the ability to intimidate others. In other words, individuals utilize different approaches in self-presentations. Jones and Pittman (1982) present five
different approaches that people use in the presentation of self:

1. Ingratiation – Involves attempts by the individual to influence others through
such behaviors as providing favors, flattery, or conforming to expectations. In
this manner, the individual is attempting to gain the "good graces" of others so
that she is seen in a positive light.

2. Intimidation – As previously mentioned, there are many people who are not
concerned about having others like them; but instead, prefer to have others fear
them. This strategy of self-presentation is utilized to convince others that he is
dangerous. Gang members, bank robbers, and other criminals, for example, use
this ploy. A number of non-criminal types, such as the gruff boss, bodyguards,
and military drill sergeants, also use this technique.

3. Self-promotion – There is an old cliché that if a person does not promote himself, who will? The self-promotion strategy is used by people who wish to inform the public about a special skill they possess or an accomplishment they
have achieved. Self-promoters do this so that they do not live in obscurity. Self-
promotion may serve the function of informing others about individual accom-
plishments and thus create the positive sense of self they hoped for; but it may
also backfire as others may see such promotion as crass.

4. Exemplification – This form of self-presentation involves an individual's attempt at being respected for her integrity and morality. This person presents
herself as the standard bearer of morality. Utilizing such an approach can be

very dangerous, especially if the person claiming to be moral has his own immorality revealed. Such is the case with former Speaker of the House, Newt Gingrich, who led a moral campaign in 1998 against then-president Bill Clinton for his alleged sexual transgressions that included cheating on his wife. Years later (in 2007), it was revealed the Gingrich was cheating on *his* wife while he led his moral crusade against Clinton. Gingrich lost any claim of being a moral exemplar once his own indiscretions were revealed. For many, Gingrich's public image is now that of a hypocrite. As Gingrich admits, "There are times that I have fallen short of my own standards. There's certainly times when I've fallen short of God's standards" (Evans, 2007:A-4). The lesson to be learned here is that, to avoid the embarrassment and shame felt by Gingrich, individuals who are not pillars of morality should not employ the exemplification strategy in their presentation of self. (In short, people who live in glass houses shouldn't throw stones.) It should also be noted that Gingrich's congressional career ended in 1998 when he suddenly resigned from Congress after being reprimanded by the House ethics panel over charges that he used tax-exempt funding to advance his political career (Evans, 2007).

5. Supplication – This strategy is often a last resort wherein the individual admits to being weak, helpless, or incompetent. This is a dangerous self-presentation strategy that can lead to great results or further damage to the self. Gingrich, like others who have cheated on their spouses, may use this strategy in seeking forgiveness from others for their individual failings. If the public accepts this plea, the individual may re-establish his or her reputation and desired sense of self. In Gingrich's case, his loyal followers quickly accepted his supplication. Celebrities like Marv Albert, Robert Downey Jr., Mel Gibson, Michael Richards, Britney Spears, and so on, who have had their images greatly compromised due to inappropriate behaviors often make very public pleas for forgiveness, admit a weakness (usually blamed on alcohol or some other drug use), and enter rehab. Generally, the public accepts such pleas for forgiveness and will afford the discredited persons another opportunity to present a more favorable self-image. In other scenarios, people who are already perceived negatively risk a more lasting blow to their sense of self because their presentation of self will never be congruent with their individual desires and the public's perception.

In sum, most people place great importance on their identity and image and they will utilize a number of tactics to avoid negative reviews from others so that they may achieve positive self-esteem. Unfortunately, no matter how hard we try, there is always great risk that our positive sense of self may be compromised by others. When this occurs we suffer from embarrassment and shame.

Among the risks confronting people that cause embarrassment and shame are degradation ceremonies. Degradation ceremonies are designed to stigmatize and compromise individual identities. Degradation ceremonies are the focus of the remainder of this chapter.

Degradation Ceremonies:
Ritualistic Behaviors Designed to Stigmatize,
Shame and Embarrass Individuals

The various cultures of the world have, throughout time, utilized a variety of approaches in their attempt to curtail the deviant behaviors of the members of society. In some instances, violators of social norms were subjected to great physical punishment, including torture (e.g., as in hanged, drawn, and quartered). Many of these ritualistic behaviors were performed in public to bring shame and embarrassment upon the violator and his or her family. In this regard, it was not enough to simply punish violators, the condemned were also meant to be degraded. As Whitman (2003) explains, "Violent punishments like mutilation and flogging are not just ways to inflict pain on people; they are also ways to degrade them" (p.98).

Around the time of industrialization, routine violent punishments were replaced by imprisonment. The primary reason for this change was a cultural belief in civility. Civil society views imprisonment as a sign of cultural advancement over physical punishment. However, despite the claim by many so-called civil societies that physical punishment is immoral, capital punishment remains as an option of castigation in the United States. Furthermore, the idea of degrading norm violators remains an integral aspect of civil society in the form of a wide variety of degradation ceremonies. And, as with the past, these ritualistic ceremonies are designed to stigmatize, shame, and embarrass individuals.

Ritualistic Behaviors

Humans are social creatures. They form groups and they interact with one another. Over time, a number of ritualistic behaviors become the norm for any group, community, or society. Rituals provide meaning and value to specific behaviors of particular social events. Elaborate rituals become a part of a greater ceremony. Many secular items begin to gain symbolic importance and are used in ceremonies. Group members internalize the value of these rituals and they become a part of tradition. In turn, tradition further empowers the importance of rituals and ceremonies. "Ritual, symbol and ceremony are not simply present or absent in the things we do; they are built in to human action. Examples of human action free of them are impossible to find, because all human action relates in some way to arenas of culturally specified significance we participate in with others" (James, 2003:7). Debernardi (2004) explains that we should not be surprised by the importance of ritualistic behavior "since ritual communication often provides actors with a metalanguage for understanding their group reflexively—its values, its hierarchy, and the sacred signs by which it represents itself" (p.107).

Degradation Ceremonies

On occasion, members of a group, community or society, can violate the dominant rules and make themselves subject to a degradation ceremony. Degradation ceremonies represent attempts by others to alter one's identity. As with any ritualistic behavior, communication plays a role in degradation ceremonies. Garfinkel (1956) states, "Any communicative work between persons, whereby the public identity of an actor is transformed into something looked on as lower in the local scheme of social types, will be called a 'status degradation ceremony'" (p.420). Garfinkel suggests that all moral societies have degradation ceremonies and only those with total *anomie* (a sense of normlessness) do not. In fact, it is highly unlikely that any society does not feature conditions and organization adequate for inducing shame. Simply put, "There is no society whose social structure does not provide, in its routine features, the conditions of identity degradation. Just as the structural conditions of shame are universal to all societies by the very fact of their being organized, so the structural conditions of status degradation are universal to all societies" (Garfinkel, 1956:420).

Degradation ceremonies are linked to moral indignation and shame. As Delaney (2005) explains, "Degradation ceremonies used at the societal level fall within the scope of moral indignation. They are designed to bring shame and guilt to the violator of the moral code. Moral indignation is equated with public denunciation. In this regard, the accused is attempting to rally the entire group into believing that the accused is guilty of some wrongdoing" (p.172). Garfinkel (1956) adds, "Moral indignation serves to effect the ritual of destruction of the person denounced. Unlike shame, which does not bind persons together, moral indignation may reinforce group solidarity" (p.421). Victims of the degradation ceremony experience a blow to their self-identity and self-esteem. Degradation ceremonies force the victims to yield to the wishes of others. "They give up control over their own moral career, finding that their fate now lies in the hands of others" (Lindersmith, Strauss and Denzin, 1991:257). Victims of degradation ceremonies are often stigmatized, embarrassed and shamed.

Stigma

As Erving Goffman (1963B) explains, stigma makes reference to a damaged self. "Stigma is a term that describes a mark of disgrace or dishonor. Persons who are stigmatized are lacking in full social acceptance, and their self-identity is negatively affected by this label" (Delaney, 2005:125). Goffman traced the origins of stigma to the ancient Greeks, who used visible signs to disgrace dishonored members of society. "The signs were cut or burnt into the body and advertised that the bearer was a slave, a criminal, or a traitor" (Goffman, 1963A: 1). Stigmas are viewed as blemishes of individual character. Goffman (1963B) explains, "We use specific stigma terms such as cripple, bastard, moron in our daily discourse as a source of metaphor and imagery, typically without giving thought to the original meaning" (p.5). Cuzzort and King (1995) conclude that "stigmata fall into three broad classes: gross physical defects, defects in character, and membership in a social class or group that is not acceptable. A stigma may be acquired at birth or at any time during the life of the individual. Although there are variations caused by the kind of stigma or the time of its acquisition, most stigmatized persons share a number of common problems and common strategies for meeting these problems" (p.337).

Stigmatized people are viewed as deviant because they have committed some type of behavior that violates the norm. In an early publication, "Embarrassment and Social Organization" Goffman (1956) states that "it is only natural to be at ease during interaction, embarrassment being a regrettable deviation from the normal state…He who frequently becomes embarrassed in the presence of others is regarded as suffering from a foolish unjustified sense of inferiority and in need of therapy" (p.264). Many people have a fear of public speaking; they blush, fumble and hesitate in their delivery, stutter, experience a tremor of the hand, sweat, and so on. Goffman (1956) believes that people who fail in public speaking not only feel embarrassed but are also stigmatized. In an attempt to conceal their embarrassment, nervous public speakers may attempt to control their performance, and sense of self and identity, by "hiding" behind the podium—they are afraid to leave the "security" a podium provides most public speakers. Goffman believed that since most people dislike feeling or appearing embarrassed, they will avoid placing themselves in such a situation. Thus, people with drinking problems should remove themselves from situations where they may be embarrassed. A drunk shaming becomes a mechanism used by others to stigmatize, and thus, alter the identity of the deviant drinker.

Embarrassment and Shame

As described in chapter 1, embarrassment is a form of social anxiety wherein a person has violated a minor social norm, committed a faux pas, or an impropriety. For example, when someone's cell phone rings in a public place, like a movie theatre, the violator will experience embarrassment because everyone will turn and look disapprovingly in the direction of the ringing phone. There is no place to hide, everyone knows whose phone it is and the perpetrator of this deviant act will be embarrassed. However, that does not mean she should be ashamed of herself because she forgot to turn her phone off and it rang. Feeling shame is reserved for violations of stronger norms. Shameful behaviors are much more intense than embarrassing ones because shame involves the violation of standards of morality.

Erving Goffman believes that the term "shame" should be applied to instances which refer to personal feelings of the actor and that the term "embarrassment" should be used when the individual's behavior is known to (or performed in front of) others. Thus, the person whose phone goes off in a public place has committed an embarrassing behavior because it occurred in front of others. On the other hand, a person who has committed some sort of immoral behavior (whether the act is known or not), such as treason or murder, should be ashamed of such behaviors because they violate major codes of morality. Miller (1996) concurs by stating that "shame has private effects that embarrassment does not" (p.22). It should also be noted that the larger the audience, the greater the level of embarrassment. The amount of embarrassment, whether embarrassment occurs at all, may depend on the size of the audience and who was in the audience. Miller argues that embarrassment will not be as severe when an infraction occurs in front of strangers (regardless of size) as it will when it occurs in front of significant others.

Goffman explains that embarrassment, whether emergent or planned, requires time, or at the very least, a number of events unfolding in a serial manner. "That is, an individual is not just mortified, embarrassed, or degraded; a set of mutually held definitions of the situation must be brought into play if an instance of self-loss is to occur. In a sense, individuals cooperate in their own mortification, and they act so as to sustain or justify definitions in which they have been judged as less than competent" (Lindersmith, et. al., 1991:255). For example, a cell phone does not randomly ring in a movie theatre. The owner of the phone did forget to turn it off. Chances are this is not the first time her phone has gone off in a public place. However, slipping on a patch of ice or freshly mopped floor is a random event, and certainly not planned. As these two examples indicate, embarrassing situations may be random or caused by the embarrassed persons themselves.

Most embarrassing incidents emerge randomly. However, there are times when embarrassment is deliberately planned. With deliberate embarrassments, "members of a group plan in advance to discredit one of their members. They may do so to facilitate socialization into a role or a preferred activity or identity—for example, hazing in the military or the college fraternity discourages one set of actions and rewards another set—or to halt the performance of an individual who is challenging the social group...Embarrassment serves as a social control device for social groups" (Lindersmith, et. al, 1991:256). As we shall see in chapter 5, drunk shamings come under the heading of unplanned degradation ceremonies, as opportunities for such shamings must present themselves and group members must be willing to "victimize" one of their friends or acquaintances. Further, Gilbert's (1998) use of the term "external shame" is applicable to drunk shamings. An external shaming occurs when people outside of an individual's immediate circle of friends become aware of the shaming incident. Internet sites dedicated to drunk shamings are filled with examples of external shame.

Historically, people have attempted to avoid shameful situations. However, in the culture of shamelessness it would appear that fewer people are concerned about the threat of being shamed as a deterrent to shameful behavior. In fact, some people will self-shame (See Chapter 4). Seemingly, in an attempt to counterattack this growing culture of shamelessness, an increasing number of social institutions are utilizing formal degradation ceremonies in attempt to reintroduce, or reemphasize, the power of shame.

Examples of Formal Degradation Ceremonies

Recall that degradation ceremonies represent a technique to control behavior. All social groups and organizations have disciplinary reviews in place to punish those who violate formal norms. The ritualistic form of punishment administrated during a degradation ceremony involves attempts to alter the identity of the norm violator. The subject of a degradation ceremony is given a label that is of lesser status than that previously held. This new label brings with it a new identity that compromises full acceptance within the group or society.

Formal degradation ceremonies are found in such social institutions as the military, the judicial system, the professional workplace, religious shunnings, the world of sports, and more. Let's take a brief glimpse at the wide assortment of formal degradation ceremonies.

Degradation Ceremonies in the Military

As one of the most formal examples of social institutions, it is not surprising that the military employs rather severe formal degradation ceremonies. The degradation process begins in "Boot Camp" where recruits are stripped of their regular clothing and mannerisms. Boot camp involves recruits going through a training process whereby Drill Sergeants degrade them while they are put through a physical and mental reconditioning program. Drill Sergeants often use insulting terms such as "maggots" and "worms" to degrade new soldiers. The entire Boot Camp process is designed to alter the identity and self-esteem of new recruits. Ideally, their self-esteem is raised upon completion of Boot Camp and the corresponding acceptance of the new identity as a soldier.

The degradation process does not end with the completion of Boot Camp. Instead, soldiers are always expected to blindly follow orders. Thinking is not necessary (akin to a McJob). Military personnel who violate the rules are subject to a formal degradation ceremony known as a "court martial."

As established under the authority of the U.S. Congress, the Uniform Code of Military Justice (UCMJ) has established a code of military laws that U.S. military personnel are expected to abide by. The Armed Forces do not have permanently established trial courts; rather, they are convened by commanders (possessing appropriate authority) on an "as needed" basis. Military criminal trial courts are known as court martials. Only military-related personnel are subject to a court martial. Court martials try "military offenses," which are listed in the punitive articles of the UCMJ and are codified in 10U.S.C.877 et seq. (Congressional Research Service, 2004).

When a service member has been accused of an offense, the accused's immediate commander conducts an inquiry into the alleged offense. If the inquiry warrants that formal charges must be pursued, the accused faces one of three general types of court martials: Summary Court-Martial; Special Court-Martial; and the most serious, a General Court-Martial. Convictions by a special or general court-martial are subject to an automatic appeal to a service Court of Criminal Appeals if the sentence includes confinement for one year or more, a bad-conduct or dishonorable discharge, death, or a dismissal in the case of a commissioned officer, cadet, or midshipman (Congressional Research Service, 2004).

The military court martial is a "classic" example of a degradation ceremony because the convicted person is stripped of a former identity (rank) and no longer enjoys the full privileges of a nondiscredited person. During the court martial process, the accused enters the military court with one rank and, if found guilty, leaves with another. The negative label of "court-martialed" is applied to the convicted person. In some cases, the court-martialed person may be labeled as a "traitor to the country." A traitor to the country is among the most damaging stigmas to be attached to one's identity. According to Shannon and Blackman (2002), Robert Hanssen, a former FBI agent, has the dubious distinction of being linked with the likes of Benedict Arnold and Samuel Mudd as being among the most notorious traitors in United States history. Hanssen leaked secrets to the Soviets for years. His betrayal is linked to the execution of at least three U.S. spies in the former Soviet Union. As the result of his degradation ceremony, Hanssen, among other things, faces being stigmatized for the rest of his life, as well as after his death.

Judicial Shamings

The judicial system, the formal social institution designed to enforce laws and appropriately punish criminals, is heavily involved in degradation. For example, the criminal courts place shameful labels such as "sex offender" on qualified offenders. These stigmatized people must register with local officials and inform neighbors (whenever they move into a new neighborhood) that they are a sex offender. Clearly, labeled sex offenders have their personal identities permanently altered and carry with them their stigma for the rest of their lives. Even in the growing culture of shamelessness, there is great disdain directed toward such shameful behaviors that lead one to be labeled a "sex offender."

Shameful or shameless behaviors on the part of political leaders may lead to a formal judicial degradation ceremony known as an "impeachment." A common characteristic of democratic societies is the allowance of a constitutional impeachment. An impeachment has two parts to it. First, an elected official must be brought up on charges. In order for an elected official to be removed from office, a second stage—conviction—must occur. Bill Clinton was impeached while serving as U.S. President, but he was not removed from office because he was not convicted of any offenses. Clinton was impeached following a chain of events which began with Paula Corbin Jones filing of a complaint at the U.S. District Court for the Eastern District of Arkansas, claiming her federal civil rights were violated by Clinton while he was Governor of Arkansas. Among other things, Jones alleged that Clinton shamelessly made unwanted sexual advances toward her. The case was dismissed in its entirety.

Clinton is not the first, nor is he likely to be the last, president to be impeached. However, there are far more citizens that face judicial sentences than there are elected officials. As a result of this fact, our attention shifts to formal degradation ceremonies carried out by the criminal courts.

Criminal courts, ideally, assure that "justice for all" prevails. Justice for all implies that innocent people accused of a crime will be freed and guilty persons will be found guilty and suitably sentenced. The penalty, as they say, should fit the crime. Under the guidelines of civility, serious crimes will lead to imprisonment, rather than torture, and less-serious offenses will allow such non-incarceration options as making restitution, paying a fine, or community service. Humiliation, of course, should never be a part of sentencing; after all, we live in a civil society, correct?

Humiliation and shaming in sentencing has been largely absent in the United States since colonial times. However, in the past decade or so, a growing number of people in the judicial system seem to feel that shaming should be a part of criminal sentencing. And a number of judges have opted for shaming sentences. Shaming sentencing allows judges an opportunity to find some middle ground between incarceration and restitution, fines, or community service. It also affords judges a chance to express their moral condemnation toward violators.

There is a growing list of examples of judicial shaming sentences (I have hundreds of examples in my files). Many of them are quite distinct. Below are few cases:

- Municipal Judge Michael Cicconetti of Painesville, Ohio certainly qualifies as a shaming sentencing judge. Among his rulings: sentencing a Painesville man who shouted obscenities (including the word "pig") at the police to stand on a high-traffic street corner with a real pig and holding a sign saying "this is not a police officer;" sentencing a woman who abandoned 35 kittens to spend the night in the woods alone without water, food, or entertainment; and sentencing an 18-year-old man who stole porn from an adult bookstore to sit outside the shop in a chair, wearing a blindfold, and holding a sign saying, "See No Evil" so that passing motorists could see him. In 2007, Cicconetti ordered three men charged with soliciting sex to take turns wearing a sign that read "No Chicken Ranch in Painesville" while wearing a bright yellow chicken costume. (Note: The sign and chicken costume are a reference to the "World Famous Chicken Ranch" legal brothel in Nevada.)
- In 2005, Oakland, California, following the lead of some jurisdictions in Texas, began plastering the faces of people who solicited prostitutes on billboards around town. This shaming program was defended as a means of fighting the exploitation of underage women (prostitutes), explained Oakland City Council President Ignacio De La Fuente. Critics claim that this shaming program is reminiscent of medieval public humiliations (*The Post-Standard*, 6/4/5). In La Mesa, California, men who solicit prostitutes may find their names on websites or billboards. In other jurisdictions, the names of men caught soliciting prostitutes are aired on "John TV" in an attempt to shame customers of prostitutes.
- Tax shaming is the rage in states like North Carolina, Maryland, and Washington as the names, addresses, and amount of taxes owed are posted on such websites as "CyberShame," "Debtor's Corner," and "Caught in the Web."
- In Boston, men who miss child-support payments have found their photos displayed on subways and buses. In London, parents who fail to pay child support are "named and shamed" on the Internet (Shipman, 2006).
- A drug user in Florida had to place an ad in the local newspaper that read: "I purchased drugs with my two kids in the car" (*USA Today*, 9/1/04).

- The state of Ohio requires judges to brand convicted drunk drivers with a special "scarlet letter" license plate—with red numbers on a yellow background so other motorists will know exactly what they have done. Other states, such as Georgia and Minnesota, use a special combination of numbers of letters. Not only are police able to identify these people, other motorists are able to mock them. Critics worry about the innocent spouse, friend, child, or parent, of the driver who uses the "scarlet" car.
- In 2005, Tennessee passed legislation requiring convicted drunken drivers to wear orange vests reading: "I am a Drunk Driver" while doing 24 hours of roadside trash pickup (Redhage, 2006).
- In November, 2006, the *Tennessee Tribune*, a black weekly newspaper, took a page from the classic "The Scarlet Letter" by affixing an "A"— for apathy—on individuals who didn't cast ballots during the August primary in an attempt to "shame them into voting" on Election Day.
- In September 2006, the police busted up a toga party at the University of Massachusetts. James Connolly, the host of the party, was charged with under-age drinking, making too much noise, and having a keg without a license (who knew you had to have a keg license?!). As part of his punishment, Connolly was made to wear his toga in front of the police station (*The Economist*, 10/12/06).
- A man who stole mail in California was made to wear a sandwich board outside a post office that read, "I stole mail. This is my punishment." After he complained that his punishment was cruel and unusual, the Ninth U.S. Circuit Court of Appeals upheld the shaming and ruled that the unusual sentence was for the purpose of rehabilitation and not just a form of public humiliation (Egeiko, 2004).
- The judicial system is assisted by the media in a variety of ways, including covering shameful punishments. For example, every time someone is charged, or arrested, for a criminal offense, the name, age, and address, of the accused appears in the newspaper, and in some cases on the radio and television news. However, seldom is the same coverage provided if the charges are dropped against the accused. That person has been stigmatized unjustly.
- Celebrities that have been sentenced to some type of community service shaming can expect to have their every move recorded by the media. Such was the case in 2007 when model Naomi Campbell was sentenced to five days of community service. Her shaming involved cleaning a Manhattan (NY) sanitation garage. Campbell's embarrassment was compounded by the media filming her every public move.
- A judge in Georgia, Sydney Nation, believes that incarceration is the wrong type of punishment for recreational drug users. In one instance, the judge ordered a defendant found guilty of possessing cocaine to serve just six months of a seven-year sentence in jail. However, upon release, the defendant was ordered to keep a coffin in his home until the seven-year period ended. The judge wanted to shame the drug user into

realizing that his drug-induced behavior was leading him to an early
death.

- Beginning in late 2006, the Raleigh, NC-based Spanish-language
  newspaper *La Conexion* has been publicly shaming Hispanics arrested
  on charges of driving under the influence of alcohol. In North Carolina,
  Hispanics make up a disproportionate number of drunken driving ar-
  rests and deaths so it is the hope of *La Conexion* to curb these shameful
  behaviors via a formal shaming (Maguire, 2007).

Proponents of judicial shamings argue that such degradation is a good way
to re-instill communal values and offset the growing culture of shamelessness.
Proponents argue that simply paying a fine or making restitution for violating a
norm pales in comparison to the shame and embarrassment that wrongdoers are
exposed with a sentencing shaming. This point coincides with the previous discussion about "guilt" as an aspect of shame. Paying a fine allows the offender to
quickly remove feelings of guilt; whereas a shameful punishment reinforces the
seriousness of the shameful behavior (norm violation) committed. Proponents
also argue for shaming sentencing (in some cases) instead of incarceration because such an innovative sentence is cheaper than the costs associated with imprisonment. Judge Cicconetti, for example, does not offer shaming sentencing
for violent offenders. He also claims that none of the people he has sentenced to
a shaming punishment has ever returned to his court (for committing a crime).

Opponents to shaming sentencing argue that such treatment is dehumaniz-
ing and akin to the days of stocks and pillories. Civil rights groups argue that
shaming sentencing violates the Eighth Amendment protection against cruel and
unusual punishment. It should be noted, however, that most judges only subject
a violator to shaming in conjunction with an option between a shaming and a
traditional punishment. Most violators choose the shaming option over imprisonment or paying a fine (*USA Today*, 9/1/04).

In cases involving non-violent offenders, shaming sentences would appear
to be a viable option to incarceration. Shaming also appears to be a strong deterrent to other would-be criminals. After all, if you saw someone standing outside
a store wearing a giant sandwich board stating "I Stole From This Store"
wouldn't that sway any possible intent of stealing from that store? Judicial
shamings are on the rise and seem to enjoy public acceptance. These sentences
are designed to shame offenders and serves as further evidence that the rising
culture of shamelessness is not free from resistance.

Workplace Shamings

There are a wide variety of formal workplace shamings conducted by persons of authority. These include, but are certainly not limited to, "workplace
mobbings" and shameful punishments for those who violate workplace rules and
etiquette.

Individuals in the workplace are sometimes targeted by others ("higher
ups") for termination for reasons that are not related to poor job performance. In
extreme cases, one may become a victim of a "workplace mobbing." The term

"mobbing" is used here in the same sense as "bullying" or "ganging up" on a victim by others to harass and intimidate. A workplace mobbing is a sinister form of psychological abuse conducted through innuendo, intimidation, harassment, badgering, humiliation, degradation, and rumor. Mobbing victims are usually exceptional individuals who demonstrate intelligence, competence, creativity, integrity, accomplishment and dedication (Davenport, et. al., 2005). The hallmark of a workplace mobbing involves the personal degradation of the target and attempts to place great stigma on the victim (Leymann 1990; Leymann 1996). Workplace mobbings are typically carried out politely and nonviolently and the participants of the mobbing are so convinced of the rightness of their campaign that they justify their attempts to shame the victim.

Workplace mobbings occur in the academic world when professors are passed over for tenure for reasons other than their job performances (for example, higher ups are threatened by the victim of the mobbing because the victim's work performance outshines that of the mob). Rather than raise their standards to meet those of the competent victim, the workplace mob attacks the "shooting star" because he or she is perceived as a threat rather than a valuable asset. In academia, not only is the victim of the mobbing shamed, but his or her students are short-changed from the opportunity of being taught by a prized professor.

In many professional workplaces, it is common for groups of employees to target another employee who is perceived as a threat. Generally, victims of workplace mobbings are not aware of the mob's degradation attempts until it is too late. In too many cases, unfortunately, victims of the workplace mobbing are left in shock by the shameful behavior of their colleagues. They are left to wonder how people could possibly perpetrate such a shameful behavior against someone who has demonstrated competency. In many cases, the mobbing victim is left questioning his or her skills in the workplace. Ideally, victims of a workplace mobbing will shine in their next work environment.

Another interesting aspect of the workplace is proper attire. Decades ago, many professional worksites adopted a "casual Friday" or "dress down Friday" policy where employees are allowed to dress less formally on Fridays. The basic idea is that such a policy somehow increases morale at the worksite. This is a fascinating concept. If morale is low at a worksite, can simply dressing casually on Friday change the collective attitude of workers? If this were really true, then wouldn't "Casual Thursday and Friday" policies double the morale of the workplace? Patrons of professions that allow employees to dress casually on Fridays have mixed feelings about such policies, as it is sometimes difficult to distinguish between employees and the clientele. Furthermore, just what is "casual" attire? Initially, it meant workers did not have to wear a suit, but over time, workers have dressed increasingly more casually. In fact, at some professional worksites women began wearing beachwear-style clothing like sandals and tank tops and men began wearing t-shirts and sneakers—and they did so without feeling embarrassed for their unprofessional dress. (Will Ferrell satirize this on a *Saturday Night Live* skit by coming to work with his buttocks exposed.) However, just as with many other liberal policies that have come under attack, the conservative mantra of dressing professionally has become in vogue once again.

Many workplaces that once allowed employees the "casual" dress option have now banned such a policy. The liberal culture of shamelessness meets the conservative backlash yet again.

In Bangkok, Thailand, police authorities have taken the shaming route as a form of workplace punishment to heart. Thai police officers who break formal rules (e.g., are caught littering, parking in a prohibited area, or arriving to work late) are forced to wear hot pink armbands featuring "Hello Kitty"—the Japanese icon of cute. Wearing such an armband is considered a mark of shame, according to senior police officer Col. Pongpat Chayaphen. Chayaphen states, "Simple warnings no longer work. This new twist is expected to make them feel guilt and shame and prevent them from repeating the offense, no matter how minor" (*Post-Standard*, 8/7/7: A-2). What's next? Will fire-fighters found guilty of violating workplace rules be made to fight fires in pink boots and raincoats?!

Religious Shunning

Close-knit communities demand strict adherence to communal norms. In some situations, individuals who violate communal law are subject to a "shunning." A shunning is a sanction, or punishment, often associated with religious communities. A person who is shunned may be avoided (as a form of behavior modification) within the community or excommunicated from the community. Those removed from the community carry with them great shame. They are social isolates who have been discredited. Shunned individuals are usually classified as a "sinner" or "traitor." The primary purpose of a shunning is to shame the target and the effects on the shunned person can be devastating. In extreme cases, a shunning may be akin to psychological torture.

Among the contemporary American religious groups to partake in shunning community members who violate communal rules are the Amish. Shunning is not only important to the Amish; it is the focal point of its split with the more moderate Mennonites. The Amish argue that they must have the right to shun those in the religious community who do not keep the faith. Many people outside the Amish community view shunning as a violation of basic human rights. But generally, unless civil laws are violated, the outside courts are unable to intervene on behalf of the shunned person. An interesting case of a shunned Amish woman in Kentucky, however, did involve a possible violation of civil rights in 2005. In this case, a woman who left the Amish community was refused service by an Amish thrift store owner. The woman claims that her civil rights have been violated; the store owner, however, claims that serving someone excommunicated from the church would be a serious moral offense (Schreiner, 2005). This presents quite a dilemma. Does one group's ideal of morality supercede the laws of the land, which guarantee civil rights for all of its citizens? What do you think? Is the Amish community guilty of shameful behavior? Or is the shunned woman guilty of shameless behavior?

Sports Shamings

Shamings in sport can be both formal and informal. A number of informal (player-initiated) sports-related shamings, such as initiations and hazing, are discussed in chapter 3. Here, we are concerned with formal shamings and degradation ceremonies found in sports. Formal shamings may begin from the time an aspiring athlete first tries out for the team. Not making the team can be very humiliating, especially if the names of the players "cut" from the team are posted publicly. Athletes that make the team must deal with the potentiality that a number of things may go wrong, including making blunders such as dropping the ball, running in the wrong direction, missing an assignment, forgetting the rules, forgetting how many time-outs the team has remaining, and so on. And in some cases, these miscues are caught on tape and replayed in the media as "blooper" clips.

Athletes are also subject to formal shamings from game officials. For example, in football, the game officials throw bright yellow flags on to the playing field to indicate that a player has made a mistake. The player that commits the infraction will have his name and/or number announced publicly. When players make mistakes in baseball, they are shamed by the Scarlet "E." The "E" of course, stands for "error." The player is identified by position as in "E-6," which means that the shortstop made an error. And in soccer, players who violate the rules are shamed by yellow and red cards waved in front of their face by an on-field official. A red card means that a player has been ejected and cannot be replaced by another player. A yellow card must precede a red card. A yellow card is a caution for improper behavior. Two yellow cards equate to a red card.

High profile athletes, especially professional athletes who are "cut" (released by the team) usually have their names printed in a variety of publications which often leads to embarrassment and perhaps shame.

Perhaps the best example of a formal degradation ceremony involves the 2005 Congressional Hearings with Major League Baseball (MLB) and the National Football League (NFL). These two highly popular North American sports leagues were called to task by Congress's Government Reform Committee because of alleged rampant steroid use among their professional athletes. Although a number of athletes were questioned, the primary purpose of these hearings was exploratory, rather than accusatory; there were a number of shameful behaviors revealed. For example, former MLB player Jose Canseco reaffirmed allegations of rampant steroid use in professional baseball. (Note: Canseco's 2005 "tell-all" book *Juiced* is filled with shameful stories.) Rafael Palmeiro vehemently denied during the hearings accusations that he had used steroids. He emphatically pointed his (index) finger at the members of the Commission to emphasis his innocence while stating, "I have never taken steroids." A couple of months later, Palmeiro tested positive for steroids. He was suspended for ten days and vilified by the public as a liar. Palmeiro's reputation has taken such a beating that this once "sure thing" athlete to make it the Major League Baseball Hall of Fame now faces the realization that his shameful behavior (lying and cheating—by taking steroids) has cost him his reputation indefinitely.

Barry Bonds continues to have his name linked to steroid use. His creditability, along with such former stars as Mark McGwire and Sammy Sosa, has been greatly compromised because of alleged steroid use. As a result of the Congressional hearings both MLB and the NFL have adopted tougher steroid testing and enforcement policies that will lead to stricter punishment. MLB Commissioner Bud Selig believes that the shame and embarrassment of being exposed as a steroid user will serve as a deterrent for players in the future.

Shame, Shame, Shame, Everywhere is Shame

Despite the growing culture of shamelessness, a number of people face life situations that compromise their sense of self and personal identities. Consider the following as a mere sampling of people facing compromised life situations that result in negative self-concept and/or shame as the result of some formal social institution.

- People living in shelters are depressed over the fact that they have little control over their lives and experience an overwhelming sense of powerlessness from the very moment they enter the shelter (Arrighi, 1997).
- Specific mental health officials have the authority to perform degradation ceremonies that may lead to someone being labeled "insane."
- "Dead-beat" fathers (and mothers) who have their photos publicly posted by Child Services as a means of degradation.
- The degradation ceremony of priests being defrocked.
- Grocery stores that display "bounced" checks as a matter of store policy.
- Schools that publicly post academic "class standings" so that all students (and parents) can see everyone's scores. (Note: Many schools have done away with class rankings because of self-esteem concerns.)
- Teachers that shame students by such methods as posting students' grades by name (rather than an ID number) and punishing talkative students by placing clothespins over their upper and lower lips—as was the case in Amanda, Ohio by a substitute kindergartner teacher.

As demonstrated in this chapter, there are clearly a large number of formal degradation ceremonies still in operation today. These ceremonies are designed to humiliate, embarrass, and shame people. People shamed by agents of formal social institutions are likely to take time to reflect upon their shameful behavior. Unfortunately, because of the social institution that shamed them in the first place, "discredited" persons may not be given a chance to regain their self-esteem and thus regain full acceptance within the community.

In chapter 3, we will learn that there are a number of informal shamings as well. Informal shamings are conducted by those not acting in an "official" capacity. The popularity of informal shamings would appear to indicate that people find joy in shaming others.

Chapter 3

Informal Shamings:
The Joy of Shaming Others

"A man who has depths in his shame meets his destiny and his delicate decisions upon paths which few ever reach"—Friedrich Nietzsche (1844-1900)

In *The Simpsons* episode "There's Something About Marrying" (#345), Bart Simpson and his best friend Milhouse Van Houten attempt to prank Barney Gumble, the Springfield town drunk, with a beer inside a trap. But Barney is wise to the mischievous behaviors of the two boys and successfully avoids being shamed by them. Bart comments to Milhouse, "We need someone new we can prank." At that moment, a turnip truck drives by (full pun intended by *The Simpsons* writers!) in front of Bart and Milhouse and a man falls off the back of it. The man's name is Howell Huser. Howell introduces himself to the boys and explains that he is a traveler who likes to learn about local folklore. Bart and Milhouse quickly realize they have the perfect foil to fulfill their need to shame and embarrass an innocent person for their own shameless joy.

Huser falls victim to one prank after another. The boys laugh hysterically at his follies. Howell is so humiliated and upset with Bart and Milhouse that he "shames" them. Shaking his hand with the index finger raised (the "classic" shaming gesture), Howell looks at Bart and states, "Shame on you." He then turns to Milhouse and proclaims, "And shame on you." Howell turns away from the boys and aims his shaming gesture toward the various Springfield buildings and yells, "Shame on your whole ill-mannered town." While Howell is shaming the entire town he points toward a group of Springfield's tough kids, Jimbo, Dolph, and Kearney. They overhear everything Howell is spouting and they do not take too kindly to being shamed. Dolph angrily points out, "My self-esteem sure didn't need that."

Sensing impending danger, Howell turns away from the tough kids and begins to run away. They taunt Howell by saying things like, "Loser" and "Get out, shamer." The rowdies throw rocks at Howell who is saved when the same turnip truck, which is now heading out of town, drives by. Howell jumps on the back of the truck and makes the other "classic" shaming gesture of rubbing one index finger over the other, toward the whole town of Springfield as he rides away. Bart comments, "I don't think we'll be hearing from him again." Ah, famous last words! A few days later, while the Simpson family is watching television, Howell Huser appears on the Soft News Network. Huser is actually a news reporter for the network who tours small towns and writes fluff stories about his travels. He is clearly still upset and blasts Springfield in his report. Howell gives Springfield his lowest score ever, six out of ten. As a result of Huser's media shaming, Springfield's tourism suffers tremendously.

What is an Informal Shaming?

The introductory story above provides many key aspects of informal shamings to be discussed in greater detail in this chapter. First, unlike formal shamings, which are instituted by representatives of social institutions and/or formal organizations, informal shamings may be instituted by anyone, even ten year-olds like Bart and Milhouse. Informal shamings, such as pulling pranks on people, are designed to embarrass the intended victims. The victims of shamings, like Jimbo, Dolph, and Kearney, often experience a blow to their self-esteem. On occasion, some informal shamings may become public via the media; for example, when the victim of a prank is Howell Huser and he reveals the shameful behavior of the youth of Springfield on television. Furthermore, as demonstrated by Bart and Milhouse's actions, another key aspect of informal shamings is the apparent joy that they bring to the perpetrators.

Informal Shamings: Quasi-Degradation Ceremonies

As discussed in chapter 2, formal shamings are akin to degradation ceremonies. Recall that degradation ceremonies represent attempts by others—in an official capacity—to alter the identity of a targeted person(s). Just as nearly all societies and formal organizations feature schemes designed to bring about shame to those who violate certain moral codes and/or social norms, so too do most social groups engage in some sort of informal behaviors that are designed to shame group members who violate expected codes of conduct. Similar to formal degradation ceremonies, informal shamings contain elements of moral indignation, shame, stigmatism, and attempts to compromise the victim's self-identity and self-esteem. However, because informal shamings are conducted without any sort of "official" representation, they may best be viewed as quasi-degradation ceremonies. (Note: The term "quasi," as used here, means: "as if," "approximately," "similar to," or "almost like.")

Informal shamings may be conducted by nearly anyone in any given social environment. For example, have you ever said something embarrassing in front of others? Most of us have. As soon as we uttered the regretful words we feel a sense of embarrassment and self-shame. We hope that others in the audience will let it pass and not draw attention to our gaffe. We feel ourselves becoming increasingly self-conscious and aware. The color of our cheeks begins to flush and inevitably, someone in the audience decides to conduct an informal shaming by pointing and yelling, "Look! His face is turning red!" This comment is usually followed by gawking audience members who laugh at the shamed person. The shamed person turns a bright red and wishes he could run and hide his embarrassment. Drawing attention to someone blushing is generally regarded as a shameful behavior but it is the person who was targeted by this comment that will feel the most shame and embarrassment.

Pointing to someone who turns red after saying something embarrassing and then making a joke at his expense is an example of an emergent, unplanned informal shaming because such an opportunity has to present itself. On the other hand, there are also planned informal shamings, such as when a group of people get together to conduct an intervention. Interventions involve friends and family members coming together at a planned time and place, but in an informal capacity, to draw attention to the self-destructive behavior (e.g., substance abuse, eating disorders, and gambling addiction) of a targeted person. When done properly, an intervention is an effective way to get people to seek help. Some people may wonder whether an intervention really qualifies as a shaming. When we realize that the primary purpose of an intervention is to draw attention to the targeted person that her behaviors are destructive and counter to the norms of the group and that those involved with the intervention *are* trying to alter the identity of the targeted person, it is safe to refer to interventions as a type of planned informal shaming.

Let's take a closer look at interventions from the perspective of Jerry Seinfeld. In the *Seinfeld* episode "The Pez Dispenser" (#31), two different interventions are discussed, one rather frivolous, the other more serious. In each case, the similarities between interventions and informal shamings are revealed. In this episode, Elaine runs into an old acquaintance, John Mollika. Elaine inquires about another mutual friend of theirs, Richie Appel. John informs Elaine that Richie is messed up on drugs and he doesn't know how to help his friend. Elaine suggests an intervention. An intervention involves gathering the target's (in this case, Richie) friends in a room and then confronting the person into going into rehab. John likes the idea of an intervention but insists that Jerry must be included, because Richie respects him.

Later, Elaine discusses the intervention idea with Jerry. After talking with John, Jerry agrees to host the intervention at his apartment. John and Jerry arrange to have Richie's friends meet at Jerry's apartment so that they can confront him on his destructive behavior. The day of intervention has arrived and all of Richie's friends are in Jerry's apartment. Before Richie shows up, Kramer, Jerry's next door neighbor, walks into the apartment. Kramer has recently joined the "Polar Bears Club," a group of cold water enthusiasts who take an annual January 1st dive into the cold New York waters. As it turns out, Kramer may also be the one responsible for Richie turning to drugs in the first place. Two years earlier, Kramer had encouraged Richie to pour a bucket of ice cold Gatorade over the head of their 67-year-old softball coach, Marty Benson. Coach Benson caught cold, got pneumonia, and died a month later.

Looking for Kramer, a number of his new-found Polar Bear buddies walk into Jerry's apartment and inquire whether or not there is a party going on. Jerry informs them that it is not a party, but an intervention. Jerry explains that a buddy of his is on drugs and they are confronting him about his harmful behavior. One of the Polar Bears acknowledges that they too have to perform the occasional intervention when one of their members stops coming. He describes how a group of Polar Bears will go to his house and say, "What, you don't want to be a Polar Bear anymore? It's too cold for you?"

Kramer's Polar Bear buddy provides an excellent example of an informal shaming utilized by many friendship groups. Belonging to a group such as the Polar Bears is a voluntary decision. The only recourse group members have to try and "force" group norm compliance is to mildly shame individuals. The line, "What, it's too cold for you?" represents a frontal attack on the Polar Bear's toughness. How can a true Polar Bear not respond but to jump in the cold waters?!

As for the more serious intervention story, Richie and John enter Jerry's apartment. Richie is taken aback by all his friends being there. He asks, "So, what's going on?" At first, Richie is hostile toward the group's confrontation and intrusion into his personal life. He does not like his sense of identity and morality being challenged. Richie feels that his friends are trying to embarrass him. Suddenly, as Jerry retells the story, Richie picks up his Pez Dispenser and becomes hypnotized by it. Richie breaks down and tells his friends about a childhood trauma. Before long, Richie agrees to go to rehab. The informal quasi-degradation ceremony has been successful. Richie's friends have made him aware of his destructive (and thus embarrassing and shameful) behaviors and he has agreed to attempt to regain his old, more positive, identity. In classic *Seinfeld* manner, this episode concludes with Richie becoming hooked on Pez while in rehab!

The Joy of Shaming Others: Schadenfreude Surrounds Us

Informal shamings are very prevalent. They are popular because people seem to enjoy informally shaming others. Finding joy at the expense of others is an aspect of the concept of "schadenfreude." By definition, schadenfreude means to gain satisfaction, pleasure, or joy at someone else's misfortune. Schadenfreude is most often associated with taking joy at the misfortune of a friend or close associate. I have described one of my favorite references to the concept of schadenfreude previously in *Simpsonology: There's A Little Bit of Springfield in All of Us!* Schadenfreude is a primary topic in *The Simpsons* "When Flanders Failed" episode (#38). In this episode, Homer Simpson's next door neighbor and sometime nemesis, Ned Flanders, is opening up his own store, The Leftorium. As a left-hander himself, Ned is all too aware of how most products are created for the convenience of right-handed people. For example, try driving a standard automobile, Ned states. Homer is already jealous of Ned and wishes that his store goes out of business. Sure enough, The Leftorium is a complete failure. No one is buying Ned's merchandise. Ned fears he will go bankrupt and begins selling all his personal items. Homer takes great delight in Ned's suffering; the viewing audience is introduced to the concept of "schadenfreude" when Lisa, Homer's daughter, explains the origin of this word. Lisa informs her father that schadenfreude is a German word for "shameful joy," or taking pleasure in the suffering of others. Not quite understanding the concept of schadenfreude, Homer discounts Lisa's explanation and explains that he is simply glad to see Ned fall flat on his butt.

Schadenfreude is an aspect of the growing culture of shamelessness. After all, wishing ill will toward friends you are jealous of violates one of the core principles of friendship, mutual respect. The American version of schadenfreude involves laughing at someone's misfortune. *The Simpsons* character Nelson displays the pleasure he experiences observing other people's suffering with his regular uttering of "Ha-ha" after someone's misfortune.

Whether it involves schadenfreude or not, chances are everyone has been victimized numerous times by some sort of informal shaming. Informal shamings begin early in life. For example, when a child misbehaves he or she is subjected to a "timeout." A "timeout" involves the child being socially isolated from others (e.g., being sent to one's room or made to sit in the corner of a room) and instructed to contemplate the misbehavior that led to the timeout. A timeout is meant to draw attention to improper behavior while the punishment is intended to embarrass the offender. Clearly, the perpetrators of the timeout are attempting to alter the identity of the offender. That is, the parent who is punishing the child for misbehaving hopes that the embarrassment of the timeout will serve as a deterrent to the child and any desires he or she may have to misbehave in the future. If other family members or friends of the family witness the child serving a timeout, the embarrassment is increased and the offending child's self-esteem takes a blow. In an effort to restore a positive sense of self, or identity, the child should learn that in order to avoid future timeouts, she must not misbehave again.

Children, like adults, are also subject to informal shamings from their peers. Neighborhood kids playing a game may mock and tease a child who does not fully understand the rules of the game. For example, some kids who play t-ball have a rudimentary knowledge of the game of baseball. In order to save them the embarrassment of swinging at and missing a pitched ball, the child is allowed to hit a stationary ball placed on a batting tee. After the child hits the ball everyone (parents, other kids, and the coaches) yells, "Run!" The confused child may run in any direction other than first base—in many cases toward third base. Even at the t-ball age, this child may be subject to ridicule for not knowing the rules of the game. Certainly by the time a child reaches the next level of baseball he or she will be mercilessly shamed for running in the wrong direction. Other errors in judgment and performance, such as dropping a routine fly ball, will also lead to informal shamings.

Having had their self-esteem shattered while playing sports at a young age, some kids may opt to avoid future sporting activities. However, this is the wrong lesson for children to learn, as informal shamings may occur in all spheres of social life, including the classroom, the cafeteria, and during recess. One may recall the old cliché, "Sticks and stones may break my bones, but words will never hurt me." This expression has a great deal of relevancy to informal shaming. Being hit by a thrown stick or stone may cause great physical harm to the victim; conversely, the argument goes, words do not carry the same weight of pain. Because this cliché has been over-analyzed for decades now, we all realize that words may also be hurtful. This is not meant to imply that words themselves cause physical pain like sticks and stones do; but rather that words may cause a great deal of emotional pain. By the time most children reach school age they have learned that certain words cause discomfort to those around them. Some will intentionally and shamelessly use specific words and expressions to cause harm to others. The victim of nasty comments is often left feeling embarrassed, shamed, and perhaps angered. Among the hurtful words people use in an attempt to shame and embarrass others are: "slut," "whore," "retard," "moron," "redneck," "hick," "cooties," and a slew of other words that may include racial and ethnic slurs.

Both children and adults may be subject to name-calling. Name-calling is nothing new, but the constant use of words that once led to someone having their mouth washed out with soap is now a part of popular culture and the growing culture of shamelessness. We try to embrace the mantra that "words can't hurt me" because it is a defense mechanism designed to protect our self-esteem. As Meaghan Morris (2006) explains, "When someone pelts words at us to try to hurt our feelings, we block them with a ritual formula that vows they will never succeed. [Saying] 'Names can never hurt me' means *you* can't hurt me—who cares what you think? Your insults are powerless; you don't matter, and I am stronger than you are'" (p.205). Thus, even though we may indeed be hurting inside, we will not give the perpetrators the satisfaction of knowing that their words hurt us. We do this to try and minimize any joy the perpetrators may experience while attempting to shame us with their words. (Note: Words *can* hurt us, as we shall see later in this chapter.)

There is a great deal of evidence to suggest that people enjoy watching others being shamed. Many television shows center on the idea of people being mildly to severely embarrassed. *Candid Camera* is a classic example of a television show that places ordinary people in everyday life situations with a twist that generally leaves the "victim" feeling embarrassed. Meanwhile a studio and television audience laughs at the victim's embarrassment. MTV's *Boiling Points* is a more extreme version of *Candid Camera*. In *Boiling Points*, professional agitators are sent out to public places to annoy people. One episode, for example, involves a person being set up on a blind date with a woman (the MTV agitator) who is pregnant and still smokes. If the victims keep their cool after a designated period of time they receive $100. However, if they blow their cool (by calling the police or swearing) they are publicly humiliated on national television. Rewarding people for not losing their cool, as MTV does with *Boiling Points*, while being humiliated, certainly adds to the culture of shamelessness because people are not reacting as they should. Specifically, people should react negatively when others are trying to humiliate them or violate their personal space.

People find so much enjoyment in watching the follies of others on television that numerous other shows such as *Punk'd, Girls Behaving Badly,* and *The Jamie Kennedy Experiment,* also air variations of informal shamings for the enjoyment of others. The culture of shamelessness continues to grow.

Can There Be a Culture of Shamelessness If We Enjoy Shaming Others?

The fact that people enjoy shaming others gives credence to the theory that there is a growing culture of shamelessness. Enjoying the embarrassment and shame of others is in itself shameless. We have reached a point in time in "civil" society where people are openly discussing whether or not public executions should be aired on television! Syndicated columnist Kathleen Parker describes the video of Saddam Hussein's hanging in 2007 as the number 1 item on Technorati, the Internet search engine that indexes more than 55 million blogs (Parker, 2007). Saddam's hanging, available online with the mere click of a mouse, was viewed by millions of people. Some people argue that executions performed at U.S. correctional facilities should also be aired, if not on regular television or the Internet, then on pay-per-view television. Family members of those scheduled to be executed argue that such a broadcast is a violation of privacy rights; and at the very least, it is shameless to suggest that executions be aired. As Parker (2007) states, "Watching someone die—especially at the hands of the state—takes us several steps backward into a time when people gathered in the public square to watch a man swing at the end of a rope. For reasons that bear examination, human beings have not needed much encouragement to swarm to the gallows. Or, as now, to click" (p. A-8). It is interesting to note that some family members of Timothy McVeigh's victims did watch McVeigh's execution.

The answer to Parker's question, "Why do human beings need little encouragement to swarm to the gallows?" has, in fact, been answered many times before. A partial explanation was provided in chapter 2, for example. Durkheim explained long ago that that public ceremonies of punishments help to strengthen communal bonds. However, in a civil society, such public ceremonies of punishments would hardly seem necessary. It is Parker's acknowledgement that we are in a culture of voyeurism that best applies to ideas of shamings. We may no longer need to go to the community square to watch someone hang, but we can now watch such behaviors from the privacy of our homes on television or via the Internet. In fact, we can view just about anything in the privacy of our own homes on television or the Internet. And much of what some people are watching involves shameful behaviors.

The shameless culture of voyeurism is a two-way street. Some people voluntarily allow themselves to be viewed by others by setting up voyeuristic computer video cams in their bedrooms (See chapter 4) while others search for people to peep in on. The voyeur is someone who gains joy from watching, especially secretly, other people's bodies or the sexual acts in which they perform. Voyeurs may also be fascinated by distressing, scandalous, or shameful events. Thus, voyeurism is an aspect of the growing culture of shamelessness.

Voyeurism is an element of the growing culture of shamelessness that resides in our private spheres. However, nearly all of us belong to many social groups that convene in the public sphere. Our group memberships are generally important to us and as a result we generally abide by the group's norms so that we may better fit in. Subcultural groupings are very important to us because these are groups we have voluntarily decided to join. For example, we choose which sports teams to support; we choose which political leaders to support and which political party to join; we decide which volunteer organizations, if any, we want to participate in; and so on.

Subcultural groups reinforce group norms and expectations to individual members. Individuals who violate the rules are subject to informal shamings. In an attempt to demonstrate the value of in-group membership, other groups are viewed negatively (out-groups) and may serve as targets for informal shamings. Subcultural group memberships are a characteristic of all people, young and old alike. However, it is perhaps, in high school where subcultural groups, or cliques, are most easily identifiable. Cliques are small groups of people that share common interests, often dress similarly, share a number of subcultural characteristics such as language, or jargon, and hang out with each other almost exclusively.

Think about it; every high school consists of a number of sub-groups (cliques) of students: jocks/athletes, burnouts (drug users), cheerleaders, nerds, the popular kids, and so on. (Other sub-groups include faculty, cafeteria staff, library staff, and maintenance; and, within these groups there are sub-groups of people who associate with one another.) By design, cliques are close-knit groups that limit their membership to "like-minded" people. We anxiously join cliques to help form an identity for ourselves. In this regard, sub-group membership serves a vital purpose for all individuals; after all, we all prefer hanging out with people with whom we share common interests and feel the most comfortable with. On the other hand, sub-group membership involves a value component in that out-group members are viewed negatively when compared to the in-group.

The 2004 movie *Mean Girls* helps to illustrate the subcultural world of high school and the corresponding informal shamings that dominate this social environment. In this popular teen movie, Cady Heron—played by Lindsay Lohan—enters the world of public high school after being home-schooled by her two zoologist parents while they conducted research in Africa. Having spent her entire life socially isolated in Africa, Cady feels out of place in this new environment and often compares it (in a narrative form) to the African jungles she once resided. Anyone who has moved to a new school can attest to the anguish experienced by the new pupil. Cady demonstrates this angst brilliantly. Her confusion begins in her first class as she has difficulty choosing which desk to sit at. She is warned by a couple of nerdy geek students not to sit at specific desks because they each come with certain hazards. For example, Cady is warned not to sit at one empty desk because the kid sitting in front of that desk farts a lot. Another desk is reserved for the boyfriend of a girl that Cady has already inadvertently upset. Grateful that anyone has spoken to her in a relatively friendly manner, Cady befriends the two artsy nerds, Janis and Damian. Janis is rumored to be a lesbian and Damian is openly gay.

It is the cafeteria setting that most clearly distinguishes the different cliques found at school. During lunch at North Shore High School, Janis visually points out to Cady (with an accompanying seating chart diagram) the wide variety of sub-groups in their high school. These cliques include: "art freaks," "girls who eat their feelings" (described as "fat girls" on chart diagram), "girls who don't eat anything" ("thin girls" on the chart), "desperate wannabes," "burnouts," "Freshmen," "ROTC guys," "preps," "JV jocks," "Varsity jocks," "cheerleaders," "JV cheerleaders," "unfriendly black hotties," "cool Asians," "Asian Nerds," "Mathletes" (members of the math club who participate in math competitions), "sexually active band geeks," "asexual band geeks," "desperate wannabes" and, of course, "the plastics." The "plastics" consist of the gorgeous, rich, spoiled girls who dress in nice clothing and act as though they are better than everyone else. The plastics get all the attention; they are "teen royalty." The plastics consist of Regina, their blonde bombshell of a leader; Gretchen, whose father invented "Toaster Strudels;" and Karen, "one of the dumbest girls you will ever meet."

The plastics constantly shame others. They find great joy in slamming people who are different from them. Regina is the most brutal. It was Regina who started the rumor that Janis was a lesbian. For a long time, Janis has wanted revenge against the plastics for spreading rumors about her and she thinks Cady will make the perfect pawn in her plan. Janis encourages the attractive Cady to infiltrate the group so that she can sabotage them. Cady agrees to help Janis. There's just one problem, Cady has to be invited into the plastics clique. One day at lunch, the opportunity presents itself. One of the older high school boys, Jason, attempts a crass juvenile pick-up line on Cady by asking her if her "muffin" is buttered. Cady is confused by this comment. Jason then offers to assign someone to butter her muffin. The naïve Cady is unaware that Jason is using sexual innuendo in his attempt to pick her up. His behavior is shameful and his comments are overheard by the Plastic Girls who are sitting at a near-by table. Regina comes to Cady's rescue and calls Jason a sleaze. Realizing he is no match for Regina's verbal confrontational skills, Jason backs off and claims that he was just being friendly.

As Regina invites Cady to join her group, Jason walks away. Step one in Cady's plan to bring down the plastics is a success; she has made personal contact. Cady continues to hang out with the plastics and slowly starts to act like Regina. She also begins to adopt the norms of the plastics. Among their primary rules:

- Always wear pink on Wednesdays.
- A ponytail can only be worn once a week.
- Tank tops can not be worn two days in a row.

- Ex-boyfriends of the plastics are "off limits" to the other plastics, "Because, it's like, the rules of feminism"—according to Gretchen.
- Jeans or track pants can only be worn on Fridays. (Typically, the girls wear short, in-style skirts and wear their long hair over their shoulders.)

The ultra "girlie" style of dress is a prime characteristic of the plastics. Because most of the other high school girls are not as fashion-conscious or as pretty as the plastics, Regina and her friends mock them. Sometimes the plastics embarrass the other girls to their faces and other times they do it behind their backs. In fact, as Cady is about to learn, the Plastic Girls have a rather formal method of informally shaming all the other girls in school. They use a "Burn Book."

One day after school, Cady is invited to Regina's home, a huge mansion. In Regina's bedroom—which is the master suite—Cady learns about the "Burn Book." (Note: Regina is so powerful that her wimpy parents allow their daughter to use their bedroom for her own.) The "Burn Book" is a collection of photos of girls from school wherein Regina, along with the other plastic girls, have written hilariously nasty comments about them. The "Burn Book" is the ultimate informal shaming book. If the plastics were a formal organization or a social institution the "Burn Book" might otherwise be viewed a formal shaming book. And, if entry to the book was conducted in a formal manner, it would be viewed as a degradation ceremony. However, the plastic girls have compiled this burn book for their own private amusement, and they are not, of course, a formal organization. Still, having one's photo with a caption added to the "Burn Book" might be viewed as a quasi degradation ceremony.

Cady is very comfortable with the plastics. She has learned their subtle ways of shaming others. Cady has also learned how to control people via compliments and manipulations. Janis senses that Cady is turning into one of "them" and tries to remind her about the plan to bring the plastics down. Regina notices Cady talking with Janis and later questions her about their conversation. Cady tries to cover her tracks and, while doing so, learns why Regina started the rumor that Janis was a lesbian. It seems that Regina and Janis were once best friends, that is until eighth grade when Regina started dating her first boyfriend, Kyle. Janis was jealous of Kyle because he took away her "hanging out" time with Regina. Regina interpreted Janis' desire to be with her as obsessive. She felt that Janis was too clingy—for a same-sex friend—and concluded that she must be a lesbian. Regina viewed this negatively and told all the other girls in school, assumingly in a derogatory fashion, that Janis was a lesbian. Janis was so embarrassed by this informal shaming and resulting shunning that she dropped out of school. Realizing she would have to return to school eventually, Janis changed her identity to a semi-gothic, artsy-type person, like an "Emo."

The term "emo" has multiple meanings, such as a reference to the punk rock scene, or a person who contemplates suicide. As used here, being an emo refers to an emotional state of mind. Poser emos talk about committing suicide because they like the attention it garners; but they have no intention of actually following through with suicide. Poser emos, then, are guilty of shameless behavior. The term "emo" is also applied to a style of dress where boys wear girls' clothes and girls wear boys' clothes. Because emos are preoccupied with suicide and angst, they often wear dark colored clothing. In this regard, they are sometimes viewed as a quasi-gothic.

Regina shamelessly stigmatized Janis primarily because she was uncomfortable with how she perceived Janis. In turn, Janis reacted to this informal shaming by becoming very self-conscious—to the point where she felt it necessary to totally change her identity. This shaming also illustrates how easily one's self-esteem can be compromised by spiteful words. Furthermore, Regina has picked up on a comment made by Cady, out of context, and mentions in her rant to Cady that Janis is now hooked on crack. If Regina starts to spread that rumor, people will soon believe that Janis is a crackhead. In fact, Cady inadvertently states to Regina that her calculus teacher, Ms. Norbury, is a drug dealer. Ms. Norbury would later be accused by officials for her "drug involvement" despite the fact that the entire story was made up. As it turns out, sticks and stones and words can really hurt us.

Informal shamings abound in *Mean Girls* just as they often do in real, everyday life. Sometimes we learn what others say about us behind our backs and other times we do not. In the case of the "mean girls" (which is code for "bitch"), the plastics have their worlds turned upside down when the "Burn Book" becomes public (it is too long of a story to get into here!). Everyone learns of the hurtful shaming words that were written about them by the plastic girls. *Mean Girls* reminds us that being shamed face-to-face is cruel. Learning that people have privately been shaming you is also hurtful.

Shaming Others Informally Through the Use of Practical Jokes and Pranks

Practical jokes and pranks represent both verbal and physical attempts to informally shame others. They are conducted when the perpetrator envisions a humorous outcome at the expense of another. Victims of practical jokes and pranks are not always amused by the tactics of pranksters. For example, I once had a friend who loved to pull practical jokes on others while in a crowded bar. He was the type of person who would set up his friends to be embarrassed by saying (loud enough to be heard by everyone in the immediate area) such things as, "Tim, she is not *that* fat!" On another occasion, he pinched a woman's butt who was standing directly in front of me and then turned away so that the woman assumed it was me. This led to a slap to my face. It also led to the end of a friendship!

Shameful Practical Jokes: "Sorry that your house burned down"

When someone tells a joke, they rely on words to "paint a picture" so that the listening audience can attempt to envision the situation being portrayed in the joke. Practical jokes involve a type of humor where the jokester actually does something; meaning there is an act or a "practice." Doing "something" physical involves a "set-up" or deception which is eventually revealed to the victim. The target then is made to be the butt of the joke and he or she is thereby made to feel foolish, or humiliated. While jokes may or may not be cruel or mean, there is an inherent strain of malice in most practical jokes (Delaney, 2008). For example, telling someone on vacation that their house just burned to the ground is not nearly as funny as it is malicious.

The introductory story to this chapter involves a reference to a *Simpsons'* episode whereby Bart and Milhouse execute a number of practical jokes on Howell Huser, an unsuspecting tourist to Springfield. These jokes were pulled in an attempt to embarrass Huser. Pulling practical jokes and pranks are a long-running theme on *The Simpsons*. For example, in "The Springfield Connected" episode (#126), Homer pulls a practical joke on his neighbor, Ned Flanders. Homer strings "Police Line Do Not Cross" yellow tape around the Flanders' home. When Ned returns home from grocery shopping and sees the police tape he immediately thinks the worse. Ned states, "Oh my Lord. Something horrible has happened." Emerging from behind a bush, Homer (laughing) tells Ned, "Fooled you, Flanders. I made you think your family was dead." Homer continues to laugh, but Ned does not find the humor in the "joke." Although Homer has attempted to humiliate Ned, it is he who acts shamefully. Anyone who attempts to find humor by making someone else believe that their loved ones are dead has clearly committed a shameful behavior.

Pranks: "Is Seymour Butts Here?"

As with practical jokes, pranks are designed to embarrass unsuspecting others. Pulling a prank is an informal way of shaming others. Nearly everyone has pulled a prank, whether it involves using some sort of device, such as a whoopee cushion, fake lottery tickets, fake dog poop, mild electric zappers, fake flowers that squirt water, rude invitation cards, novelty dirty diapers, and so on; or making a prank phone call. Prank phone calls, sometimes called crank calls, are generally harmless. Examples include: ordering 10 pizzas to be delivered to someone's home, calling a grocery store to see if they have "Prince Albert" in the can, selecting a random phone number and asking the homemaker if their refrigerator is running, etc.

Certain types of prank phone calls, however, can jeopardize the safety of others. For example, calling a 911 operator to report a false accident can divert emergency services away from real emergencies. Such was the case in South Glen Falls, New York. An 8-year-old girl (named withheld from news reports) placed 135 prank phone calls to 911 operators. The juvenile prankster called to report false accidents, leading officers on wild goose chases. Sheriff's deputies and 911 dispatchers used surveillance equipment that trace cell phone calls using satellite technology. The deputies traced a prank call to the girl's home while she was on the phone with a 911 operator (*The Post-Standard*, 2/10/07).

In the early years of *The Simpsons*, it was quite common for Moe the bartender to be the victim of a prank phone call, usually perpetrated by Bart. The prank phone calls utilized in *The Simpsons* are inspired by the famous recorded prank calls from the *Tube Bar* tapes, the first of which were released in the early 1980s. Louis "Red" Deutsch, a no-nonsense type of guy, opened the *Tube Bar* in Jersey City, New Jersey, after Prohibition. His legendary short-temper made him an easy target for prank phone calls from John Davidson and Jim Elmo (who released the tapes). The pranksters would ask "Red" to call out fictitious names, which, when said aloud, sounded like something else. As soon as Deutsch would catch on to the prank he would respond with extreme hostility. "Red" shouts obscenities (mostly "mother" insults) at the pranksters, threatening them with bodily harm if he ever found out who they are (Delaney, 2008).

In *The Simpsons*, *Moe's Tavern* serves as the *Tube Bar*, and hot-tempered Moe represents Deutsch and his short fuse. In the early *Simpsons* episodes, it was common for Bart to make prank calls to *Moe's*. For example, in the "One Fish, Two Fish, Blowfish, Blue Fish" episode (#24), Bart asks Moe if there is a Seymour Butts at the bar. Moe yells out to the bar patrons asking for a Seymour Butts. He states, "Hey, everybody, I wanna Seymour Butts!" After it finally dawns on him that he is being pranked, Moe threatens Bart over the phone. Moe claims that he will pull out the eyeballs of the prank caller with a corkscrew.

In the "Principal Charming" episode (#27), Bart pranks Moe by asking if Homer is there. Moe repeats the question by asking "Homer who?" Bart quips, "Homer Sexual." Once again, Moe checks with the bar patrons asking if anyone there is Homer Sexual. Once again it dawns on Moe that he has been pranked. And again, he threatens bodily harm on the phone prankster.

In every case where Bart calls Moe he manages to embarrass and shame him. But prank phone calls have mostly fallen out of favor these days as phone calls can easily be traced. Someone needs to use a pay phone—if you can still find one—to best assure not being found out making a prank phone call.

Spaghetti Trees and Left-handed Whoppers: Embarrassing Others on April Fool's Day

April Fool's Day, or "All Fools Day" as it is sometimes referred to, is a prankster's favorite holiday. April 1st is the one day of the year where nearly any type of prank or practical joke can be instituted under the protection of the "April Fools!" disclaimer.

The origin of April Fool's Day is commonly believed to be traced back to the 1500s when the Gregorian calendar took over from the Julian. Those who forgot to acknowledge the change and attempted to celebrate New Year's Day on the previously celebrated first day of the year (April 1st) were teased as "April Fools." The people who embraced the new calendar mocked (shamed) the traditionalists (those who refused to accept the new calendar) and sent them on "fool's errands" in an attempt to trick them into believing something else that was false.

The primary intention of an April Fool's prank is to play a joke on an unsuspecting person(s). The trickster attempts to set up a scenario wherein the targets are led to believe a false claim is true. In many cases, these tricks are borderline cruel. For example, a married person telling her spouse that she wants a divorce; telling someone that a mutual friend has died in a car crash; or a boss telling one of his employees that he has just been fired. Proclaiming "April Fool's!" is hardly proper compensation for what the victim has just experienced. This helps to explain why many people do not look forward to April Fool's Day. On the other hand, many April Fool's jokes are clever and harmless. Classic gags like changing the time on the clocks, placing plastic insects on someone's chair, or saying it's snowing outside when it is really 70 degrees are relatively non-threatening attempts to embarrass someone. In some cases, an April Fool's joke may be quite exciting and positive. For example, I heard of a family having a large gift box delivered to a woman on April Fool's Day 2007. The woman did not know what to expect when she opened it. Upon opening the box the woman screamed. But these were screams of joy as her son—who was serving in Iraq—had made a surprise visit home. (Note: Other family members helped to put the gag together.)

In early April 2007, a number of news outlets were reporting that Keith Richards of the Rolling Stones had admitted to snorting cocaine mixed with bits of his father's cremated remains. Richards reportedly stated, "He [Richard's father] was cremated and I couldn't resist grinding him up with a little bit of blow" (*The Post-Standard*, 4/4/7). A spokesperson for the Rolling Stones late admitted that Richard's comments were nothing more than an April Fool's Day joke. "It was an off-the-cuff remark, a joke, and it is not true. File under April Fool's joke," said Bernard Doherty (*The Post-Standard*, 4/5/7).

The joy of shaming others on April Fool's Day has been given special attention by the online site, Museum of Hoaxes. This website (see http://www.museumofhoaxes.com/hoax/aprilfool.com) has compiled a "Top 100 April Fool's Day Hoaxes of All Time" list. Here is a sampling:

- At number 22 is "Arm the Homeless." This April Fool's Day hoax involves a 1999 *Phoenix New Times* article announcing the formation of a new charity to benefit the homeless. Typically, fundraisers designed to benefit the homeless are centered on providing food and shelter. However, this charity would provide them with guns and ammunition. The story was covered by a number of news outlets including *60 Minutes II*, the Associated Press, and a number of local news media before they finally realized they had been punk'd. (Originally, this prank was perpetrated by students at Ohio State University in 1993.)
- At number 8 (and my personal favorite) is "The Left-Handed Whopper" classic prank pulled by Burger King in 1998. Burger King placed a full page advertisement in the *USA Today* announcing the introduction of a left-handed Whopper made especially for left-handers. According to the ad, the new Whopper would include all the same ingredients as the original Whopper but all the condiments were rotated 180 degrees for the benefit of left-handers. Reportedly, thousands of people went to Burger King specifically asking for the "Left-Handed Whopper" not realizing the joke. Some people requested the regular "right-handed" Whopper fearing that the new Whopper would not taste as good as the original.

- The number one April Fool's Day joke of all time, according to the "Museum," is the "Swiss Spaghetti Harvest" perpetrated in 1957 by the respected BBC news show *Panorama*. In this report, it was announced that Swiss farmers were enjoying a bumper spaghetti crop. Footage of Swiss peasant women picking strands of spaghetti from trees was also shown during this "news" broadcast. Thousands of viewers were suckered into believing this hoax and wanted to know how they could plant their own spaghetti tree. The BBC diplomatically replied that people should "place a sprig of spaghetti in a tin of tomato sauce and hope for the best." (This footage can be found on the BBC's website.)

Undoubtedly, many readers have their own favorite April Fool's Day stories. The thread that links them all is that the targets of these pranks are supposed to be embarrassed and shamed. The fact that so many people enjoy conducting pranks and practical jokes on others reflects the notion that many people find joy in shaming others.

The Role of the Mass Media and the Internet in Shaming

Most likely, humans have always pulled practical jokes on one another. By comparison, and thanks to technology, many of today's pranks and shamings are far more elaborate. The perpetrators of informal shamings have the various forms of media and the Internet to thank for this. Furthermore, the media itself is involved in informal shamings.

Mass Media-related Shamings

Providing news, information, and entertainment is the trademark of the contemporary mass media. The term "media" refers to all communication relays and technologies (Real, 1996). The word "mass" refers to a large audience. Put together, the mass media becomes the medium by which large numbers of people are informed about local, national, and international events. The mass media consists of television, radio, motion pictures, newspapers, books, magazines, and sound recordings. Traditionally, the mass media has been viewed as forms of communication that permit a one-way flow of information from a source to an audience. However, today many forms of media allow for a two-way flow of communication. For example, some television shows allow fans to interact with programming via cell phones or the Internet. For now, the Internet remains in a category all to itself and separate from the mass media.

Nearly everyone uses and enjoys many aspects of the media. Most people watch television (Americans averaged an all-time high of 4 hours and 35 minutes per day in 2007), go to the movies, listen to sound recordings, or read some form of print publication on a regular basis. Inevitably, aspects of the media become accomplices to, or perpetrators of, informal shamings.

In many smaller newspapers, it is fairly common for individuals to be shamed by friends and family members. For example, in one of the newspapers I regularly read I glanced at a photo of an individual who has, apparently, just turned 40-years-old. Family members of this man sent to the newspaper a silly photo from his childhood. The caption to the photo read, "Lordy, Lordy, Look Who's Turned 40!" Although the birthday of this gentleman is being celebrated, he must endure mock shaming by having an unflattering photo of himself placed in the local newspaper available for all to see. The use of the local newspaper allows for a far more effective informal shaming than if the photo was only viewed by the immediate family and friends at his birthday party.

In more extreme cases, people may be informally shamed by a much larger segment of the mass media. For example, who has not heard of Jennifer Wilbanks, the "Runaway Bride"!? Wilbanks was scheduled to marry her fiancé, John Mason, on April 30, 2005 but developed "cold feet" and shamelessly ran away from home a few days prior to the ceremony. Fearing for her life, Mason called the police, suspecting foul play. Her worried family posted a reward for her safe return. Realizing that people were looking for her and in an attempt to thwart Mason's efforts to find her, the thirty-two-year-old Wilbanks called her fiancé and shamefully claimed that she had been kidnapped and sexually assaulted by a Hispanic male and a white woman. Hundreds of police officers and volunteers searched for Wilbanks for three days until she was eventually found. She had never been kidnapped but shamefully clung to her story about being abducted until her story finally fell apart. Wilbanks was charged with a felony for filing false information to police. She was later sentenced to two years' probation and 120 hours of community service and ordered to pay restitution to the Gwinnett County Sheriff's Department.

The media had a field day with Wilbanks and dubbed her the "Runaway Bride." Stand-up comics used her for the butt of their jokes for weeks. Numerous derogatory terms were thrown at Wilbanks. For example, many people said that Mason was lucky not to marry this "nutcase." Sticks and stones...

Just as we thought this story had run its course the "Runaway Bride" saga returned to the media in a rather unique form of informal public shaming. In 2007, the Albuquerque Police Department used this shameful event to promote a recruiting program. Billboards around Albuquerque showed a female police officer, Trish Hoffman, gently apprehending a woman in a wedding gown wearing running shoes underneath a caption that states, "Running away from your current job? Call APD Recruiting 343-5020." It was Officer Hoffman who escorted Wilbanks through the airport with a blanket over her head two years earlier. The image of Hoffman and Wilbanks was shown on television and appeared on newspapers across the country. The billboard image also appeared in newspapers across the nation.

The shameful escapade of Wilbanks has been immortalized by (among other things) a "Runaway Bride" action figure and a hot sauce called "Jennifer's High Tailin' Hot Sauce."

Newspapers, the leading source of reliable news information, not only provide facts; they also allow readers to express their opinions in the "Letters to the

Editor" section. Newspaper editors also share their opinions on the "Editorial" page. It is the editorial page that allows readers to determine whether the newspaper has a liberal, moderate, or conservative slant to the news. Occasionally, editors are so passionate about a particular issue that they allow staff writers to voice their opinions in a series of articles; often, with the lead story appearing on the front page. For example, in 2006, England was in the midst of a scandal involving the perceived leniency of many of Britain's top judges dealing with sex offenses and other serious crimes. *The Sunday Times* and *The Sun* ran a "shaming" list of judges they perceived as being too soft on killers, pedophiles, and violent thugs. The June 11, 2006 *Sunday Times* included a front-page article caption: "'Lenient' Judges Shamed in List." The article, written by Steven Swinford and Daniel Foggo (2006), was designed to shame judges that they felt were unduly lenient on violent offenders. The more than 200 judges are named on a "shaming list." Meanwhile, *The Sun* printed photos and brief descriptions of the most "shameful" judges under the caption: "*Sun* Campaign: Judges on Trial." The word "Guilty" appears in large font size in the midst of the shameful judges' photos.

Although newspapers may be viewed as formal organizations, their role in shaming the judges was conducted in an informal forum. Add to this the purposive intent of the newspapers to embarrass the judges, and we have an informal shaming. Presumably, the editorial staff took pleasure (joy) in shaming judges that they felt were not doing their jobs properly.

Embarrassing others in newspapers is just the tip of the iceberg of examples of media-related shamings. Sound recording artists, such as Eminem, Alanis Morissette, No Doubt, Guns-N-Roses, Ratt, and Carly Simon are among the many who have attempted to informally shame musical rivals and past lovers in their music.

In 1973, Carly Simon's number one hit song "You're So Vain" dominated the charts. (The song is from Simon's 1972 *No Secrets* album.) The lyrics clearly reflected her feelings about being spurned by an ex-lover, alleged to be Warren Beatty, Mick Jagger, or former fiancé William Donaldson. Simon claims that the song is not about any one person but rather, a composite of a number of ex-lovers. (Note: Beatty believes that the song is about him.) The lyrics in one stanza reveal how embarrassed Simon was by being dumped. She claims to have been young and naïve and duped by this former lover; ultimately stating that her dreams were akin to clouds in her coffee.

Simon's description of being dumped by an ex-lover actually represents a type of self-shaming, as most people would attempt to keep such intimate details private. However, it is the "Refrain" that shifts the focus of the intended shaming to another by claiming her ex-lover is so vain that he probably thinks this song is about him.

Obviously, since Simon wrote a song about an ex-lover dumping her, the lyrics are about him! What other conclusion could one reach? Well, there is the attempted informal shaming motive of Simon's to cleanse her hurt feelings by shifting the burden of guilt to another. Instead of taking responsibility for her relationship's failing—due to her own possible shortcomings—Simon attempts

to shift the blame of her shame to the ex-lover's vainness. This concept reinforces the idea that informal shamings are a self-esteem coping device. After all,
it is easier to move on in life if one blames another instead taking the blame for
one's shortcomings.

In the appropriately named Ratt song, "Shame, Shame, Shame" (from the
1990 *Detonator* album), another ex-lover is publicly and informally shamed in
the form of musical lyrics. The lyrics to the opening stanza tell the story of a
cheating lover making moans and groans and nasty laughter so loud that they
can be heard outside closed doors.

The chorus to "Shame, Shame, Shame" reflects the hurt and embarrassed
feelings that any person may experience after they realize that their lover has
cheated on them. In this case, the spurned lover has the forum to informally
shame the shameful cheater. The cheating lover is told that she has no one else
to blame for the break-up but herself and that it is now time for her to feel the
pain—of break-up. Shame, shame!

The spurned Ratt lover was so incensed over being shamed by his cheating
ex that the band not only wrote the song "Shame, Shame, Shame" as the second
song of the *Detonator* album; its first song (an instrumental) is titled, "Intro to
Shame."

Undoubtedly, a countless number of songs have been written to informally
shame others, but few are as blatant as Simon's "You're so Vain," Ratt's
"Shame, Shame, Shame" or Alanis Morissette's "You Oughta Know."

The greater the audience size, the greater the ability to shame someone in
the media. Further, the "bigger" the celebrity status of the media person attempting to publicly shame others the greater the likelihood someone will be shamed.
Thus, few young people today have heard of Carly Simon or Ratt, but undoubtedly, they have heard of Don Imus and Howard Stern.

Imus and Stern are among a growing number of people in the media who
informally shame others. Generally their targets are celebrities, political figures,
and other people making the news. Publicly poking fun at others in the form of
insults and jokes are a trademark that Imus and Stern share. Howard Stern's
comments were considered so "outrageous" that the Federal Communications
Commission (FCC) was constantly monitoring his behavior. He was subjected
to fines and suspensions as the result of the FCC's crackdown on "indecent"
commentary. In response to constant censorship, Stern left the public airwaves
(which are governed by the FCC) for the unregulated satellite airwaves in 2006.
Before Stern left for satellite radio, he was the self-proclaimed "King of All Media." Unfortunately for Stern, millions of his listeners did not follow him to the
unregulated atmosphere of Sirius radio. This left the door open for long-time
shock-jock Don Imus to reclaim his throne atop commercial talk radio.

Enjoying great success and millions of listeners, Don Imus was taking great
pleasure in his lofty position as a CBS syndicated (to more than 70 stations
around the United States) radio host whose program was also simulcast on
MSNBC television. By design, Imus infuses questionable language and commentary within his edgy, often non-politically-correct show. He frequently tests
the mantra that "words cannot hurt me." For example, Imus has referred to

Senator Hillary Clinton as "bitch" and Howard Kurtz, a *Washington Post* media critic, as a "boner-nosed, beany-wearing Jew-boy." In fact, he has offended, among others, numerous athletes, politicians, and media celebrities. On April 4, 2007, Imus discussed the NCAA Women's Basketball Championship game between the University of Tennessee and Rutgers University. He then offended the Rutgers players, eight of whom are African Americans, by shamelessly saying, "That's some rough girls from Rutgers. Man, they got tattoos..." His producer Bernard McGurk added, "Some hardcore hos." Digging himself in a bigger hole (no pun intended), Imus quipped, "That's some nappy-headed hos there, I'm going to tell you that." Imus and his producer both laughed at their own shameful comments. Imus' producer also compared the women to the Toronto Raptors, an NBA (male) team.

The fallout from Imus' shameful behavior was quick and costly. He was condemned by the National Association of Black Journalists, the National Organization for Women (NOW), the Rutgers Women's Basketball team, and millions of outraged citizens. Shortly thereafter, Imus was fired by CBS Radio. However, because he had just signed a new five-year deal with CBS Radio, Imus threatened a breach-of-contract lawsuit against his former employer. They offered him a lucrative settlement.

Many people remain offended by the racist and sexist nature of Imus's comments. "Nappy" is generally considered an outdated term used to describe the small, tightly curled hair that is a feature of many African Americans. (Most African Americans have their hair straightened out to avoid this look.) Using the word "nappy" is considered derogatory when referring to a black person's hair. Although it is interesting to note that just a few weeks after Imus made his infamous comments about nappy hair, *American Idol* contestant LaKisha Jones (an African-American woman) referred to her own childhood hair as a "nappy 'fro." She had made this comment during her retrospective following her boot from the show on May 9, 2007. (She had made it to the final four.) Oddly, the media did not make a big deal about her comment. Pointing the shaming finger is often a selective process.

The word "ho" is short for the word "whore." The term "ho" is used regularly by many people in popular culture, especially those in the "hip hop" and "rap" communities. Nonetheless, calling a group of women "hos," and nappy-headed hos on top of that, on a nationally syndicated talk show is deemed highly shameful and offensive as evidenced by the fact that both MSNBC and CBS fired Imus within 8 days of his initially making the comments. All his apologies were ignored and the growing culture of shamelessness was confronted by a coalition of people who demand a certain level of morality by public figures who have access to a large media audience. It should be noted, however, due mostly to his one-time high level of popularity, Citadel Broadcasting Corp. announced in November 2007 that Imus would be on the air hosting the morning drive time on New York based WABC-AM starting December 2007.

Howard Stern is no stranger to the culture of shamelessness, as he is a proud contributor to this movement. The negative tone of his show is centered on mocking, shaming, and degrading a litany of people. His exploits have been well documented by others, but now that he has exiled himself to satellite radio, Stern is all but an after-thought for most people. Seldom do we hear of Howard Stern any longer, as satellite radio has yet to achieve "the next big thing" status as predicted by the radio shock jock. In early 2007, Stern made headlines for aligning himself with the website *votefortheworst.com*. This website is designed to shame the highly popular *American Idol* television show that allows viewers to vote for their favorite singing Idol. The shameless Stern encouraged his listeners to visit the "Vote for the Worst" website and vote for Sanjaya Malakar, a clearly less-talented singer. Whether it was a coincidence or not, round after round, Malakar somehow survived the weekly elimination rounds as more talented singers were voted out of the competition. He would reach the "Final 7" before finally receiving the least number of votes. Rest assured we have not heard the last of Sanjaya Malakar.

Internet Shamings

Increasingly, many aspects of the media overlap. As already mentioned, commercial radio shows are sometimes broadcast simultaneously on television and nearly all radio and television stations maintain active websites. In this regard, radio talk show hosts can describe an event and create an online link for their listeners to view at a later time. In some cases, the links take users to photos or short videos are people in embarrassing situations. However, it is not just members of the media using the Internet to informally shame others. Many individuals have taken it upon themselves to shame others online. In fact, there are so many stories of online informal shamings that it would be impossible to cover them all. But, here are a few examples that readers may find of interest:

- A Philadelphia-based Comcast Corp employee, who was making a house call to a replace a customer's modem, fell asleep on the customer's couch while on-hold for more than an hour with his own company. Now, while it is embarrassing for Comcast that their own employees are put on hold for an hour, let alone customers, the brunt of the shame was endured by the sleeping employee. The Comcast customer filmed the sleeping employee and then posted a 58-second video of the incident on YouTube.com, a site that lets users share videos (Hart, 2006).
- A jealous husband discovered his wife having an affair with a college student and posted the sexually suggestive correspondences between the two. The husband did not use their real names, but instead their online screen names. A large number of Internet surfers stumbled across this informal shaming and, using detective work, discovered the true identities of the cheating wife and college student. These same Internet users tracked down the college student and took turns harassing (shaming) him in his classes and off-campus.
- A Queens, New York teenager, named Sasha, learned the hard way that crime does not pay. The teenager's mother purchased a cell phone from someone on the street who had found the lost cell phone of a woman

named Ivanna. Upon learning that her cell phone was lost, Ivanna sought the help of her computer savvy friend, Evan. The lost cell phone contained a Sidekick with a built-in camera. Sasha took photos of herself and friends. Apparently, she was unaware that Ivanna had access to copies of all the photos. Eventually, Evan was able to track down Sasha's email address and MySpace page. He asked Sasha to return the phone to its rightful owner, but she refused. Next, Evan set up a website where he shamed Sasha's behavior by posting all the photos that Sasha had taken on Sasha's MySpace page. Numerous people wrote Evan in support. In addition a number of viewers began to harass Sasha and her family at their apartment building and yelled "thief" in front of her neighbors. Evan simply wanted to retrieve his friend's cell phone, but Sasha would not relinquish it. Eventually, the police arrested Sasha and charged her with possession of stolen property. The cell phone was returned to Ivanna. Amateur detective Internet users went on to their next case.

- A growing number of women riding the subway in New York City have taken justice into their own hands. They are fed up with gropers and flashers intruding on their personal space and rather than hoping for the police to do something about it, they are taking photos of the shameful men's behavior. These photos wind up, you guessed it, on the Internet!
- In California, a news story about a woman who gave birth to a healthy child just two days after learning she was pregnant led the new mother to being victimized by a relentless number of people posting shameful comments on the Internet. The postings insulted the woman for being so heavy (she weighs nearly 400 pounds) and for having a messy house. The shameful postings including such comments as, "A pig is a pig." Once again, it should be pointed out, words *can* hurt someone.

Internet informal shamings are becoming increasingly popular. They represent a type of "cyberspace justice" where people can anonymously, or openly, vent their frustrations with others in a public forum. If Internet users have sympathy for their cause, those seeking cyberspace justice may even gain an army of vigilantes willing to shame those who have shamed others. There is every indication that we have witnessed merely the beginning of "cyberspace shaming justice." Purveyors of shameful behavior, watch out!

Informal Shamings in Sports: Initiations and Hazing

The sports world is filled with examples of informal shamings. Sports writers, for example, often write scathing articles on social issues in general and certain athletes in particular. Rick Reilly, a regular contributing writer for *Sports Illustrated*, describes a shameful incident that occurred in 2006. A high school athlete in Texas, who was arrested and awaiting trial on six counts of aggravated robbery with a deadly weapon (each of which carries a sentence of five years to life if he's convicted) was allowed to play football as long as he wore his court-ordered ankle monitor. The coach at his original high school has a policy of not playing guys who are out of jail on bail; in fact, this coach has kicked guys off for missing practice! But as Reilly (2006) states, "Luckily, in this country, where shame is on a permanent holiday, there are bleachers full of football coaches willing to give youngsters facing six-count felony charges another chance. Especially youngsters who are all-district" (p.72).

Perhaps the most common form of informal shaming involves teammates, at all levels of play, mildly mocking each other when someone goofs up on the playing field. Generally, teammates tease one another in order to help alleviate the pressure of the game. They find joy with informally shaming each other. Teammates also informally shame one another as a means of strengthening group cohesion. Group solidarity is accomplished when all the members view each other as relative equals. One of the most common methods utilized to reinforce group cohesiveness involves some sort of initiation or hazing.

Many groups attempt to instill group camaraderie via an initiation or hazing. The military, fraternities, police and fire departments, and street gangs, all utilize some form of initiation or hazing as a rite of passage into full group membership. Because initiations and hazing ceremonies sometimes lead to personal injury, or in rare cases, death, most social institutions do not formally allow such practices. This does not, however, stop member participants from engaging in these quasi-degradation ceremonies.

By implication, initiations and hazings are far more common in team sports than they are with individual sports. The targets of these ritualistic ceremonies are first-year players. Shortly after the player makes the team, he or she is subjected to a potentially intense ritual, the initiation. The naming of this ritual as an "initiation" is quite logical in that it is derived from the word "initiate" which means to begin, or start, a new course of action or behavior. An initiation is a rite of passage, a long-held tradition of most institutions that marks entrance, or acceptance, into a group. Initiations are a common aspect of the sports world. Most of these initiations involve shaming; in some cases these shamings are so damaging to the athlete's self-esteem that they quit sports. Snyder and Spreitzer (1978) noted this shaming process three decades ago when they stated, "It is clear that many normal persons are turned away from sport for a lifetime as a result of experiencing degradation ceremonies during their childhood or youth" (p.64). Initiations may involve such behaviors as having the athlete run around the field naked, or partially clothed; taping the athlete to a football goal post; a physical beating; performing menial, or degrading tasks; and hazing.

Hazing generally operates under the cloak of secrecy. Perpetrators and victims of hazing seldom admit to their involvement in hazing events. The secret nature of hazing serves as a bonding experience among the participants. Those who initiate the hazing ceremony have already experienced the victimization of hazing, which allows them to easily justify victimizing newcomers. Newcomers who successfully survive their hazing experience look forward to the day when they become hazers. And thus, the cycle perpetuates itself while simultaneously justifying itself within the group setting.

Unfortunately, many people who have undergone a hazing quasi-degradation ceremony are permanently scarred from the experience. These scars may be visible or hidden internally. (This is analogous to victims of mental abuse whose scars may not be visible, but are just as real as physical scars.) Internal scarring is the result of the humiliation and shaming aspects of hazing. With this in mind, Crow and Rosner (2004) define hazing as "any activity expected of someone joining a group that humiliates, degrades, abuses, or endangers, regardless of the person's willingness to participate" (p. 200).

Hazing rituals, the extreme version of an initiation, have been formally restricted at nearly every high school and college. Over the past few years, an increasing number of hazing incidents have come to light due to their online postings. In this regard, some hazings resemble the drunk shaming ceremonies, in that such shameful behaviors have been going on for centuries. But with the advent of the Internet these previously private ceremonies have become more public. And when hazing photos become public, it is up to school officials to formally punish those responsible. The current trend against hazing in high school and college sports is most likely to continue. This trend represents yet another attempt to thwart the growing culture of shamelessness.

Will The Joy of Informally Shaming Others Continue?

As demonstrated in this chapter, there are numerous forms of informal shamings. They may be perpetrated by family members, friends, sports teammates, the media and users of the Internet. Generally speaking, people seem to find great joy in mocking others, as we all seem to take pleasure in the follies of others. Informally shaming others is joyful to people because it gives them a mild boost to their self-esteem. That is, most people feel better about themselves if they can be positively compared to others.

Furthermore, as the culture of shamelessness continues to grow, we can expect to witness a corresponding increase in the number of informal shamings by those who resent this cultural shift in morality. However, the cultural moralists have a struggle ahead of them; as of today, it has become increasingly common for people to not only joyfully shame others, but joyfully shame themselves. In the next chapter, the growing phenomenon of self-shaming is explored. Undoubtedly, we will find joy in informally shaming them as well!

Chapter 4

Self-shamings: Degrading One's Self

"The only shame is to have none"—
Blaise Pascal (French mathematician, philosopher and physicist, 1623-1662)

Some time ago, I attended a wedding. The traditional and solemn ceremony was held on an early Saturday afternoon in a church more than one hundred years old. The bride looked stunning in her long white gown and the groom looked equally handsome in his well-pressed tuxedo. The bride and groom exchanged heartfelt vows to each other. And when the ceremony was complete, the groom eagerly followed the priest's urging of, "You may now kiss the bride."

As dictated by custom, a huge wedding reception followed the nuptials. All the guests were in good spirits and happily greeted the newlyweds. The sit-down meal was accompanied by an open bar. As anyone who has ever attended an event with an open bar can attest, there is bound to be someone who drinks to excess. In this case, it was the best man (the brother of the groom) who helped himself to a little too much libation. He was already quite intoxicated by the time he was supposed to make the toast and fumbled humorously through his speech. Although a few of the guests were mildly upset with his lack of ability to behave properly, no harm was done. However, as with a number of the other guests, the best man continued to drink heavily. He then decided to hit the dance floor, where his lack of dancing skills were on full display for all to see. And, of course, in this day and age of video cameras his every move was captured on tape to be replayed over and over again.

The best man then jumped onto the stage and attempted to sing along with the band. He must have thought he was quite the singer as he loudly, and out of tune, belted out the wrong words to the "chicken dance." At the climax of his stage performance, the drunken brother of the groom fell from the stage. Although he was physically unharmed, his personal reputation took quite a blow.

The visibly upset mother of the bride reacted as though the wedding reception was ruined and approached the young man, who was still sitting on the dance floor, and sternly proclaimed, "You should be ashamed of yourself."

Explaining Self-shaming: "No Shame Is Given, If No Shame Is Received"

When someone says to another, "You should be ashamed of yourself" she is stating that the target did something wrong, or shameful. As described in chapter 1, feeling shame involves experiencing an emotion stronger than embarrassment. In this regard, the offender is viewed as being "guilty" of some sort of misbehavior. Thus, when someone clumsily falls, say from a stage at a wedding reception, he will typically experience embarrassment, but not shame. However, if this person falls from the stage as a result of being excessively drunk (such as the case described in this chapter's introductory story) many people may view such a behavior as shameful. The bride's mother was clearly attempting to affix shame to the best man's drunken behavior via verbal chastisement. She was also attempting to condemn and dishonor the best man by pointing out his disgraceful conduct.

Shame, however, can only be experienced by the alleged perpetrator if he or she feels guilty of committing a misdeed worthy of self-condemnation. Say for example that the drunken best man feels no remorse for his out-of-control behavior. If this is the case, how will he feel ashamed? As it turns out, the best man at this wedding reception refused to accept any sort of condemnation and instead, not so politely, informed the mother of the bride to "lighten up" and "have some fun!" (Surely, this has led to some interesting post-wedding reception, in-law family gatherings!) Thus, a person who refuses to feel shame when told, "You should be ashamed of yourself" has found a "loophole" in the power of guilt utilized by shamers. Specifically (and paraphrasing a U.S. military motto), "No shame is given, if no shame is received."

What is Self-shaming?

When people liberate themselves from the shackles of labels that are bestowed upon them, they are free to engage in deeds that others may render as shameful. This attitude is a prevailing sentiment in the culture of shamelessness and results in an increasing number of people who are willing to shame themselves.

People who shame themselves are, in effect, challenging the cultural norms of society. Self-shamers are telling the world that they are willing to engage in behaviors that society finds inappropriate, and they don't care about the possible consequences. If self-shamers take on key cultural expectations, however, they risk social condemnation and a compromised sense of self. Self-shaming, then, may be defined as behaviors that individuals freely engage in that run the risk of compromising one's sense of self and may result in social reprisals from others. Self-shaming generally creates a sense of excitement for the participants and their need for thrills outweighs the value of attaining full acceptability within the greater community. As a result of this exhilaration, some self-shamers may actually enjoy a heightened sense of self.

There are numerous instances of self-shaming acts; many of which are rather good-natured and relatively harmless. For example, singing at a karaoke bar with friends in front of roomful of strangers can be quite embarrassing for those who cannot sing very well. But who really cares when it is just good-natured fun that leads people to sing karaoke? Another relatively harmless example of self-shaming involves dressing in funny or provocative Halloween costumes. Halloween is the one time of year where people can dress as anything or anyone and get away with it. People do this shamelessly because they enjoy acting different from their normal selves. Wearing funny shirts with slogans and "words of wisdom" written on them can be another way of self-shaming; such as when an overweight person wears a shirt that reads: "I am in shape. Round is a shape."

Speaking of being round, a student once told me that she self-shamed by joining "Weight Watchers" and subjected herself to public weigh-ins. She admitted to gaining weight each of the three weeks she attended the meetings. She questioned why she should shame herself in front others and quit attending the diet center.

The willingness to self-shame often tests the limits of reason. Such is the case with Chicago Bears fan Scott Wiese of Forsyth, Illinois who agreed to change his name (as part of a bet) to Peyton Manning if the Bears lost the 2007 Super Bowl against the Indianapolis Colts. The Colts won and Wiese did indeed petition the courts to legally change his name to that of the quarterback who beat his beloved Bears in the Super Bowl. However, Macon County (IL) Circuit Judge Katherine McCarthy refused to approve of the name change, citing that it was "too confusing and risks infringing the privacy of the football player" (FOX News.com, 2007). It takes a special kind of person to shame himself by taking the name of an athlete who broke his heart. You will never hear of a Cleveland Browns fan willing to take the name John Elway, that's for sure!

On the other hand, some self-shaming behaviors are a little more complicated and/or risqué and lend themselves open to public condemnation. Let's examine a few examples.

Donkey Basketball: Acting Like a Jackass, But In a Good Way!

Generally, acting like a jackass will lead to condemnation from others. Then again, some people have turned acting like a jackass into a profitable adventure. Johnny Knoxville and Bam Margera are prime examples of people who have shamed themselves by acting like idiots on television and film. Undoubtedly, most readers are aware of the MTV show, *Jackass*, originally shown from 2000 to 2002, which features Knoxville, Margera, and others performing a variety of dangerous, asinine, sadomasochistic, and self-harming stunts and pranks in the effort to entertain an audience. Since 2002, two *Jackass* films have been released. Despite the fact that the majority of the population views the *Jackass* behavior of Knoxville and crew as shameful, if not ludicrous, these actors, apparently, do not experience shame.

Knoxville and Margera are ambassadors for the growing culture of shamelessness as their behavior should not be emulated by others and, yet, they are laughing all the way to the bank. Then again, Knoxville and Margera are not the first people who have attempted to make money acting like a jackass. Indeed, many schools (as well as other organizations such as police and fire departments) have encouraged their teachers and principals to act like jackasses while riding a donkey, albeit in the name of charity while participating in a sporting event.

Typically, people do not ride on donkeys while playing sports; it would, after all, appear silly and unpractical. But that is the whole point of charitable events such as "donkey basketball" or "donkey baseball." Donkey basketball, the most famous of the donkey-related sports, is a variation of the standard game of basketball, except that the participants ride atop donkeys while attempting to play ball. The participants of donkey basketball do not care about the consequences of looking silly, nor do they feel embarrassed, when riding a donkey while playing sports because the event is designed as a fund raiser. (And, apparently, the donkeys do not feel embarrassed when they poop on the court!) A number of commercial firms provide the donkeys and equipment and split the proceeds with the organization that hires them.

Audience members generally take great delight in watching otherwise dignified persons attempting to play a sport while riding a donkey. It is common for players to slip off the donkeys, making jackasses of themselves. But since this is done for charity, the self-shaming aspects are good-natured and mild in comparison to other forms of self-shaming.

It should be noted, however, that some animal rights groups consider donkey-sports as shameful. They believe that the animals are mistreated. For example, it may be necessary for the donkey handlers to whip or hit the donkeys to force them to play. Most companies that supply the donkeys argue that their animals are treated humanely and therefore the only shame involved in donkey-related sports is experienced by the participants.

Tiny Tim: Tip-toeing Through the Tulips

Johnny Knoxville and the rest of the *Jackass* crew are certainly not the forerunners of entertainers who have attempted to make a living via self-shaming. Many celebrities have made a fortune acting in a self-shaming manner. Baby Boomers will recall that Tiny Tim (born Herbert Khaury), for example, made a living via his shameless persona as a singer and ukulele player. Tiny Tim (1932-1996) gained a cult following in the Greenwich Village music scene by the early 1960s. His distinctive style was the result of oddly unique renditions of contemporary songs. According to Tiny Tim's biography, it was his appearance in the film *You Are What You Eat* that led him to a booking on the hugely popular *Rowan and Martin's Laugh-In* (1968-1973) comedy television show. *Laugh-In* embraced the hippie culture and propelled the careers of many young stars, including the adorably ditzy Goldie Hawn and the hilarious Jo Anne Worley. *Laugh-In* is credited with popularizing many famous quotes during this era, including:

> The devil made me do it
> You bet your sweet bippy
> Sock it to me
> Verrry interesting…but stupid
> Look *that* up in your Funk and Wagnall's
> Fickle-finger of fate
> One ringy-dingy

Tiny Tim's cameos fit in perfectly with this irreverent show. Tim, himself, was an odd-looking character. He was tall (about six-foot one-inch); overweight; had a large nose; and, wore long black gangly hair. Tim also played a relatively small-sized ukulele. His "trademark" song was "Tip Toe Through the Tulips" (from the 1968 *God Bless Tiny Tim* album); a song title that still brings a smile to the faces of those who grew up watching Tiny Tim's career.

Tim's most memorable self-shaming public appearance was his December 17, 1969 marriage to Miss Vicki on the *Tonight Show* with Johnny Carson. "Miss Vicki" was the name Tim used to describe his 17-year-old bride, Victoria Budlinger. An estimated 45 million viewers tuned in for Tim and Miss Vicki's wedding. The stage was decorated with numerous tulips from Holland. The wedding is believed to be the second highest rated show of the 1960s—the July 20, 1969 moon landing was the most watched. While Tim considered the wedding ceremony to be a dignified event, most observers were left with a feeling of embarrassment for Tim. Miss Vicki and Tiny Tim lived mostly apart during their eight-year marriage, but they have a daughter, Tulip.

Tim clung to his hippie persona (that made him big in the 1960s) throughout his career. And because of this he was often viewed as "joke" by younger generations who did not quite "get him." Tiny Tim shamelessly continued to perform until his death in September 1996.

Redneck Yard of the Week

Sometimes, entertainers provide the forum for regular folks to self-shame. Such was the case on *Blue Collar TV*, a short-lived television show hosted by Jeff Foxworthy in the mid-2000s. *Blue Collar TV* was a conservative comedy that centered primarily on Southern stereotypes; such as espousing the hillbilly and redneck lifestyle.

Among the recurring sketches that embraced the redneck mantra are the "Redneck Dictionary" and "Redneck Yard of the Week." The Redneck Dictionary involves cast members putting on a brief skit where they take common words and morph them into stereotypical redneck talk. The word of the week was shown on the television screen. For example, "artichoke." On Blue Collar TV, artichoke was used in a sentence as a means of definition, "I 'artichoke' the feller who told me to order this."

Interestingly, I looked up the meaning of the word "redneck" in the diction-ary and found the following definitions: "an uneducated bigot;" "uneducated white farm worker;" slang for "a rural white southerner who is politically con-servative, racist, and a religious fundamentalist;" an "offensive term used to describe a member of the white rural laboring class, especially in the southern United States;" and "a white person regarded as having a provincial, conserva-tive, often bigoted attitude." Wow! With definitions such as these, why would anyone want to admit to being a redneck? I doubt very much that we will hear Jeff Foxworthy utter, "If you're an uneducated bigot, you might be a redneck" anytime soon!

And yet, there are those who embrace the redneck label. A number of lo-cales sponsor redneck sporting activities. Texas plays host to the annual "Texas Redneck Games" where competitors participate in such games as the "Mattress Chunk." The mattress chunk involves two-man teams wherein the teammates toss a mattress from the back of a pickup truck as far as they can. The ugliest "butt-crack contest" is another favorite among the Texan rednecks.

Blue Collar TV provides us with yet another example of embracing the red-neck label with its sketch the "Redneck Yard of the Week." The "Redneck Yard of the Week" was a sketch where host Jeff Foxworthy and regular cast member Ayda Field showed photos of yards that a redneck would be proud to claim. Viewers sent in photos of their own yard for consideration of this award! And *Blue Collar TV* treated it like a real award. During these sketches, Foxworthy and Field, dressed in their formal best, reviewed a few select photos and an-nounced the winner as if they were at an awards show—like the Grammys. Jeff provided a mocking commentary of the "winning" yard. For people who have never seen this show, the photos usually involved a junky yard where the grass has not been cut for some time, and a number of blue-collar items were visible throughout the yard. These items included junk cars, old bathtubs, and a porch about to collapse. Often included in the photo was the "redneck" yard owner beaming proudly.

What an interesting and good-natured way to self-shame! If you think about this scenario for a moment you realize that in order to win the "award" for "Redneck Yard of the Week" individuals were willing to be publicly humiliated. First, the viewing audience learned that you cannot take care of your own yard. Second, Jeff Foxworthy would mock you and the gorgeous Ayda Field would laugh at you. And third, one must be willing to see the "redneck" label as posi-tive and not a self-shaming.

Although having a "redneck yard" is self-shaming enough and having mil-lions of people view your stigma adds to the humiliation, there are more embar-rassing situations that individuals may encounter in their lifetimes. For example, have you ever told someone, "I love you," only to be rejected? Trust me, it's no fun!

Saying, "I Love You"

When people first start to date, it is often clear to one, or both, of the dating partners whether there is any chance of a lasting future between the two of them.

There are times when couples stop dating after the first date and there are times whey they break up after a few dates. On other occasions, however, couples continue to date for an extended period of time. Generally, when this happens, the dating partners begin to develop romantic feelings for one another. Ideally, if one develops strong romantic feelings, so too will the other. People who have intimate feelings for their dating partner will inveterately express their emotions by saying "I love you." This is a bold move. Many of us have been burnt in the past and are weary about professing love to another unless we are sure of the return expressed feelings. A great example of the dangers of saying, "I love you" for the first time is provided from *Seinfeld* in "The Face Painter" episode.

In this episode, George Costanza is dating a woman named Siena. They have been dating for a while and George has developed strong feelings for her. George informs his friends, Jerry and Elaine, that he wants to tell Siena that he loves her. Jerry, sensing impending doom, asks George whether he is confident that he will receive the "I love you" return. George admits that it may be a 50-50 chance. Jerry warns George that he is potentially setting himself up for a big emotional letdown. But George tells his friends that he really wants to tell Siena that he is in love with her.

What Jerry has sensed is George's potential for a self-shaming. George has admitted that he is not sure whether Siena shares his feelings but he is willing to lay his heart out to her anyway. He has chosen to ignore the potential embarrassment he will experience if she does not express similar feelings.

The big night arrives. George and Siena are sitting in his car listening to the Devils-Rangers NHL playoff game on the radio. George attempts to set the proper mood to express his feelings by telling Siena that he could have gone to the hockey game that night but didn't because he did not want to break his date with her. Siena gives him a look like, "Are you crazy?!" But George does not pick up on this nonverbal cue. Instead, he tells Siena, "I love you." Just as Jerry suspected, Siena does not return George's sentiments and instead informs George that she is hungry and suggest that get something to eat.

Obviously, George has suffered a blow to his self-esteem. He knew that the odds were not staked in his favor but he proceeded with the dangerous affirmation, "I love you," anyway. But George is given a chance to elevate his shattered self-esteem when he learns from his friend Kramer that Siena is deaf in one ear. George now has the opportunity to tell himself that she simply did not hear him say, "I love you" and boom, his self-esteem is restored. However, George does not take advantage of this opportunity. Instead, he risks shaming himself even further. George thinks that maybe Siena did not hear him and therefore if he repeats his confirmation of love to her, maybe this time she will reciprocate. Later that next evening, George eagerly prepares himself. Once again in his car, George loudly states to Siena, "I LOVE YOU!" With a smile on his face and hope in his heart, George prepares for her answer. Alas, it was not meant to be, as Siena completes George's self-shaming experience by saying, "Yeah, I know. I heard you the first time."

Clearly, there is no comeback for that response. George's shame will lead to their immediate breakup.

Undoubtedly, there are people who are sympathetic to the George character as there are few feelings worse than the pain associated with having one's love for another go unreciprocated. But, at least this type of self-shaming does not involve a public viewing. In that regard, the shame is minimized. Other people are not so lucky, as their shameful behavior may be witnessed by a crowd. For example, there have been cases where a guy has proposed marriage to his girl-friend on a jumbo screen at a professional ballgame only to be turned down! Like George Costanza, this person feels embarrassed and shamed.

A public shaming of another sort involves a former high school student, Joseph Frederick in Juneau, Alaska. In 2002, Frederick and his friends pulled a prank that many people considered shameful. Of course, that is bound to happen when someone promotes "Bong Hits 4 Jesus."

What if God Got High?: Bong Hits 4 Jesus

Frederick, a high school student from Juneau, Alaska, decided to pull his prank during a school-sanctioned event to watch the Olympic torch relay as it passed in front of the high school (MSNBC.com, 2007). The then-18-year-old student unraveled a 14-foot banner in full public view, and in front of live TV cameras, that read: "Bong Hits 4 Jesus." Although the banner was displayed off school grounds, Frederick got into trouble because he was on a school-sanctioned field trip. Frederick has since claimed that he was not promoting religion or drug use; but rather, expressing his constitutional right to free speech.

The high school principal, Deborah Morse, confiscated the banner and suspended Frederick from school for 5 days. His punishment was doubled to 10 days after he quoted Thomas Jefferson on free speech. Frederick and Morse had run-ins prior to this incident over his previous acts of protest. The school had called the police to remove him from a common area and he was disciplined for remaining seated during the Pledge of Allegiance.

Morse was attempting to shame Frederick for his behavior by suspending him. However, Frederick believed his right of free speech was compromised by Morse's behavior. He never backed down from his claim and took Morse to court over his right to display a banner, even one that reads "Bong Hits 4 Jesus." The district court ruled in favor of the School Board and Morse but the Ninth Circuit reversed the District Court decision. The school board asked the U.S. Supreme Court to review the Ninth Circuit's decision. In June 2007, the Supreme Court endorsed First Amendment limits by ruling (5-4) against Frederick. Writing on behalf of the majority, Chief Justice John Roberts claims that schools can regulate student expression that advocates the use of illegal drugs.

The Morse v. Frederick case is hailed as one of the most important cases on student's rights to protest on school grounds since the Vietnam War student-led protests. Frederick had cited the landmark 1969 ruling of Tinker v. Des Moines which states that students do not "shed their constitutional rights of freedom of speech or expression at the schoolhouse gate." Since this ruling, the courts have shifted toward empowering schools in their right to censor free speech under the pretense of maintaining order and protecting certain students from harmful messages.

Although this story is discussed as an example of self-shaming—because Frederick brought this degradation ceremony upon himself—the more poignant issue rests with the realization that self-shamers will not experience shame if they do not perceive their behavior as shameful.

Shamelessly Baring It All

In some cultures, especially those in the Middle East, people, especially women, are expected to keep their bodies covered. This expectation of behavior is to be adhered to because of the norm of humility. In other cultures, especially Western societies, people are free to dress quite liberally, especially when situations dictate. In other words, it is perfectly acceptable for individuals to bare a great deal of skin at the beach, but they must dress more modestly at work, school, and at other public gathering places.

In the growing culture of shamelessness, however, individuals are flashing skin more freely. Visitors to New York City's Times Square have no doubt come across the "Naked Cowboy." The "Naked Cowboy" is a legendary figure who stands in the middle of Times Square wearing only underpants and cowboy boots while holding a guitar in an attempt to draw people's attention to himself. He offers to have his picture taken with tourists in exchange for a cash payment. The "Naked Cowboy" is comfortable with his own body. Are you as comfortable with yours to dress nearly naked in public? How about going *au naturel?*

Some people, in fact, are so comfortable with baring their bodies they embrace nudism, or naturism as it is often called. Although most Western societies are not so liberal as to allow open nudity, pro-nude proponents have found sanctuary at a growing number of nudist camps and beaches. There are nudist bed and breakfast inns, nudist and naturist clubs, campgrounds, and spas. Some nudist facilities are designed for swingers and romantic adult oriented vacations. Further, there are many nudist colonies that have morphed into large-scale glamorous resorts that offer a variety of amenities.

For those who have never been to a nudist resort or a nude beach, chances are, your image of such a place involves beautiful, young people frolicking shamelessly. The reality is much different from this utopian view. In fact, based on my limited experiences, the vast majority of people at nude beaches are older, overweight folks, that frankly, I do not need to see naked! But, to each their own.

The Garden of Eden vision that non-nudists conjure is more likely to be found at Spring Break beaches where young college-aged women proudly reveal their bodies, ala "Girls Gone Wild" style. Joe Francis and his production company Mantra Films have made millions of dollars filming young women who voluntarily show off their bodies and engage in soft porn actions in front of cameramen. These women sign a release form and expose their breasts and/or buttocks often in exchange for little more than a tank top, a pair of panties, or a trucker's hat.

But why are these women willing to expose themselves? As *Los Angeles Times* staff writer Claire Hoffman (2006), explains, "Francis has aimed his cameras at a generation whose notions of privacy and sexuality are different from any other. Nursed on MySpace profiles and reality television, many young people today are comfortable with being photographed and having those images posted on the Internet for anyone to see. The boundaries that once contained sexuality have also fallen away. Whether it's 13-year-olds watching a Britney Spears video, 16-year-olds getting their pubic hair waxed to emulate porn stars or 17-year-olds viewing videos of celebrities performing the most intimate acts, youth culture is soaked in sexuality." This willingness to freely engage in sexual activity, especially in public, is a key aspect of the growing culture of shamelessness.

There are a variety of reasons why someone shamelessly engages in promiscuous sexual behavior. Some simply enjoy the sex. Others enjoy the attention it brings. In some cases young women are willing to shamelessly make out with other young women in front a camera or a group of guys because one of the women may have a crush on one of the guys. She is presuming that the guy will find "girl on girl" action as "hot." And, in most cases, guys do find it hot to watch attractive young women—lesbians or not—make out.

It should be noted that exposing oneself in such a manner as the "Girls Gone Wild" girls do in a public place is often a criminal offense, but these women proudly self-shame nonetheless. Although participating in these videos is a personal choice, there are enough women who have claimed that they signed the release form while they were underaged or drunk—thus invalidating the release form—and who feel so embarrassed and ashamed of their behavior (after the fact) that they have sued Francis and Mantra Films. Although Francis could not be brought to court for making someone feel embarrassed and ashamed, he was brought to court in September 2006 for failing to document the ages of young women engaging in sexual acts in his videos, as federal law requires. Francis pleaded guilty and three months later, the U.S. Department of Justice ruled that Mantra Films must pay $1.6 million in criminal fines for violating federal law. In addition, Francis was jailed (in Nevada) in April 2007 for contempt of court. Upon his release, Francis faces possible extradition back to Florida to face trial on charges related to using minors in sexual performances and misdemeanor prostitution charges (*The Post-Standard*, 10/26/07). Thus, the courts have deemed Francis to be guilty of shameful behavior.

Youthful self-shaming indiscretions, such as those that involve exposing one's body parts to be shown on a video, is often viewed quite differently by many of these same women years later when they are married and have their own children. As we shall see in chapter 5, exposing oneself while drunk is just one type of shaming related to consuming alcohol.

A growing number of college women and men are taking their clothes off in a less public arena via nude parties. "Naked parties" are a rage at many northeastern colleges, including such Ivy League colleges as Yale and Brown. Students at Brown University claim naked parties began there back in the 1980s. Since then, the idea has caught on and spread to Wesleyan, Wellesley, Columbia, Massachusetts Institute of Technology, and Yale (Aviv, 2007). Generally, these naked parties are not sexual in orientation; rather, they involve the freeing of the body from fetters of clothing. The naked party participants generally sit around and talk, play pool, and music, and so forth.

Student groups, ranging in size from 30 to 300, organize these parties to be held in neglected rooms in classroom buildings, libraries, basement storage rooms, and other semi-secluded areas. At Yale, the naked parties are organized by a group of students known as "The Pundits" (Aviv, 2007). The Pundits are a secret society that have existed at Yale since 1884, but turned their attention to naked parties in 1995. The Pundits have a history of rebelling against Yale tradition, often via pranks. Understandably, they do not want university officials knowing their identities.

College students, of course, are not the only ones who are shaming themselves by the means of exposing themselves. Anyone is capable of doing something embarrassing. Such is the case of man found wearing a blonde wig, pink flip-flops, and a red-black-and-white striped bikini while taking a drunken afternoon romp through a park. Steven S. Cole of Mason, Ohio, a 46-year-old volunteer firefighter, told police he was on his way to a bar to perform as a woman in a contest that offered a $10,000 prize. His blood-alcohol level was twice the Ohio limit of 0.08 at the time of the arrest. Cole's lawyer explained, "He is obviously humiliated and embarrassed by the entire situation" (*The Post-Standard*, 4/6/7).

Despite one's belief that alcohol consumption and nudity may represent a wonderful marriage, as we have learned, the combining of the two often leads to embarrassing and self-shaming situations. The culture of shamelessness seems less concerned about this reality than those who are trying to counter this movement.

Self-shaming for Fame

Conservative people might have a hard time understanding why anyone would be willing to self-shame. That is, why would people voluntarily place themselves in a situation where others will judge them negatively? I have already provided a number of examples of people who have self-shamed for a variety of reasons (e.g., for charity, love, and as an expression of the right to free speech). Perhaps the most plausible explanation for self-shaming rests with the realization that the younger generation has a fascination with becoming famous. In that regard, young people are willing to engage in a variety of behaviors that are self-shaming as long as it helps them attain fame.

Research has shown that young people indicate that their generation's top life goals involve the desire to be rich and famous. They are not exactly sure how to attain that fame, but they know they want to be famous. The Pew Research Center released poll results in 2007 that reveals eighty-one percent of 18- to 25-year-olds say getting rich is their generation's most important or second-most-important life goal; fifty-one percent said the same thing about being famous (Jayson, 2007). Thus, the average young person finds it important to be rich and famous, even though the odds are drastically against them. A representative of the Pew Research Center believes that MTV and reality TV are, in large part, fueling these youthful desires. MTV, for example, has a show called, *I Want a Famous Face*. *I Want a Famous Face* follows the transformations of twelve young people who have chosen plastic surgery to look like their celebrity idols. Talk about low self-esteem and a poor sense of self!

Despite MTV's ability to find people who are willing to change their face to resemble that of someone already famous, most young people have an over-inflated value of their own self-worth. For example, today more than eighty percent of children call themselves a "very important person." This is a figure considerably higher than the twelve percent cited in a similar poll in the 1950s (Halpern, 2006). How is it, that so many youngsters have developed such an over-inflated sense of self? After all, they haven't even accomplished anything at this point in their lives and, yet, they consider themselves important. The primary explanation for this question rests with their parents and the culture of shamelessness that instills the belief that everyone should have high self-esteem and modesty be damned. No wonder so many young people believe that they will become rich and famous.

Sex Sells: Maybe I Can Appear Naked in the Media

The worlds of marketing and advertising have long known of the simple adage, "Sex sells." Young people who have grown up watching *MTV*, reality TV, and a great deal of primetime TV are exposed to an abundance of shows and advertisements that are sexually explicit. Magazines, video games, and movies often glamorize sexual situations as well. Many young people grew up watching a sweet Lindsay Lohan in *The Parent Trap* and listening to a young pop star, Britney Spears on the Disney Channel's "New Mickey Mouse Club." Parents thought it was cute that their daughters adored such sweet stars. However, as Lohan, Spears and stars like them grew up to become hot, sexpot young women, their behaviors changed correspondingly. Hardly a day goes by where the media does not discuss Lindsay, Britney, or Paris Hilton. And girls and young women emulate the styles of these celebrities. Research published in the journal *Pediatrics* indicates that for white teens, repeated exposure to sexual content in television, movies and music increases the likelihood of becoming sexually active at an earlier age. The study found that 55 percent of teens who were exposed to a lot of sexual material had intercourse by 16, compared with only six percent of teens who rarely saw sexual imagery in the media (Deveny and Kelley, 2007).

Boys and young men receive messages from the media as well. They play violent video games, watch graphic and sexually-implicit movies and TV shows, and listen to popular music, especially rap and hip-hop, which promotes the idea that it is okay to objectify women and use degrading terms such as "ho" and "bitch." When boys are exposed to this type of attitude from their male idols and women dress and act provocatively like their favorite celebrities we see how the "sex sells" attitude greatly contributes to the growing culture of shamelessness.

Celebrities and would-be celebrities have turned to the "sex sells" attitude in an attempt to make themselves more marketable. Anna Nicole Smith, for example, propelled her career by posing in Playboy. Posing in Playboy, or any nude magazine for that matter, once carried a stigma, but in the culture of shamelessness it can be a career move (forward). The "sex sells" mantra has a carry-over effect as well. In fact, sex is so marketable that it seems to carry the same weight as "any publicity is good publicity." For example, celebrities, such as Paris Hilton and the then-married Tommy Lee and Pamela Anderson-Lee, have had sex tapes of themselves leaked to the public, via the Internet, and not only did their careers not suffer, they were assisted by this free publicity.

On the other hand, some one-time celebrities are so far off the public's radar that the release of one of their sex tapes will hardly create a ripple of interest in the vast pool of celebrity. For example, Dustin Diamond, who played the character Screech on the 1990s TV show Saved by the Bell, had a 40-minute porno video of himself with two women show up on the Internet in 2006. There are allegations that the release of the tape was staged in an attempt to revitalize his waning career. Despite the idea that sex generally sells, Diamond's career was not revitalized. An image of Diamond as a self-shamer, however, lingers.

One of the most memorable examples of a celebrity sex scandal involves Vanessa Williams when she was Miss America. This former Syracuse University student was crowned Miss America in 1983; she was the first African American Miss America. However, during her reign, Penthouse magazine released nude photos of Williams posing provocatively with another woman. The September 1984 issue, which features a photo of a smiling Williams and George Burns on the cover, led to Williams' resignation as Miss America.

This shameful event was multi-faceted. First, most commentators believed that Williams' career was washed up before it had a chance to really begin. The Miss America pageant had never faced such controversy in its history. Second, Williams was devastated. She felt embarrassed by the photos and many people expressed how ashamed they were of her. Third, the photos never should been released in the first place. Williams worked for a New York photographer as a secretary and makeup artist during the summer of 1982. The photographer, Tom Chiapel, allegedly convinced her to pose nude and promised Williams that the photos were for artistic purposes only and that they would never be published. When Williams was crowned Miss America, Chiapel found an opportunity to profit from the black and white photos. Williams never authorized the release of the photos but Penthouse agreed to publish the photos after Hugh Hefner refused to allow his Playboy magazine to publish them. A fourth shameful aspect of this Penthouse issue does not involve Williams. Instead, the focus of shameful behavior rests with the magazine as their centerfold featured porno star Traci Lords. Although being a porno star is in itself an extreme form of self-shaming, Lords was only 16 years old at the time of her spread in *Penthouse*. (Note: After Lords turned 18 years old she admitted to her real age. Her porno tapes were pulled from stores.)

Williams is clearly a survivor. Despite her resignation as Miss America, she is still officially recognized by the Miss America Organization as Miss America 1984. She has gone on to establish an outstanding career as a singer and television and film star. In 2007, she became the 2,331st person to receive a star on the Hollywood Walk of Fame.

Embarrassing Moments Caught on Film: Might As Well Share Them with Millions of Strangers!

It takes a special type of person to self-shame via a sex tape. Most of us are not comfortable with the idea of our sex lives being made publicly available for consumption. However, it is also quite clear that a far greater number of people than ever before are now willing to shame themselves by sharing embarrassing home videos with complete strangers. With that in mind, a number of shows, most notably *America's Funniest Home Videos*, were created to provide a viewing audience a glimpse of others' awkward moments captured on film.

America's Funniest Home Videos (*AFV*) premiered on January 14, 1990 and is still airing today. Videos are submitted by viewers who compete for cash prizes. Meanwhile, a studio and television audience laughs at their follies. In addition, to regular weekly contests that award $10,000 for the clip the studio audience chooses as its favorite, $3,000 for second place, and $2,000 for the third-place winner, there is a special $100,000 grand prize awarded at the end of the season to the video determined to be the funniest or most unusual. (Note: Any contestant that wins first prize in a weekly show is eligible for the grand prize.) Host Tom Bergeron introduces the clips that involve funny and embarrassing moments for adults, children, animals, and sometimes even inanimate objects. (Note: Bob Saget was the original host of *AFV*.) As explained on its ABC website, *AFV* broadcasts videos that range "from practical jokes to home improvement plans gone awry, from animal mishaps to just flat out strange behavior. *America's Funniest Home Videos* pull out all the stops to present a hilarious look at everyday people caught on tape in their most embarrassing moments" (ABC.com, 2007).

AFV claims to have given away over $9 million in prize money since its inception and has evaluated more than a half a million videotapes from home viewers. Clearly, a large number of people are willing to shame themselves on television. *AFV* also invites a number of people who send in their videos to appear in the studio audience so that they can be shamed in person (although, *AFV* does not word it in quite that manner!). And of course, people are willing to do this! Ah, the growing culture of shamelessness.

As one might suspect, Americans are not the only people who are willing to shame themselves by having their home videos aired on television; numerous other countries have adopted variations of the *AFV* television show and their viewers are just as eager to self-shame.

American Idol: "She Bang, She Bang!"

The most popular American television show is *American Idol*. First airing on June 11, 2002, this annual show has provided FOX Television with Top 5 ratings since its second season. It was the number one show in its 5th (2006) and 6th (2007) seasons. *American Idol*, for the unacquainted, is a singing competition. The show attempts to discover the best young singer in the United States through a series of nationwide auditions. Because *American Idol* hopes to "discover" new talent—so that its parent corporation (19 Entertainment) can profit from the would-be American Idol—contestants are not allowed to have any current record deals or be signed to any talent agency. (Note: 19 Entertainment holds the exclusive right of refusal for management and merchandising of any Idol contestant and the singers are obligated to sign with its record company, Sony/BMG.)

During the early audition rounds, tens of thousands of *Idol* hopefuls will try out; first in front of preliminary judges and ultimately—if they are lucky—in front of the show's three primary judges. The three star judges are: Randy Jackson (record producer and bass player); Paula Abdul (former pop star); and Simon Cowell (producer and manager). The show is hosted by Ryan Seacrest. Contestants that make it through the first round are invited to Hollywood for the semi-final round, where they go through a more rigorous screening. Eventually, a Top 12 is determined. From that point on, singers are eliminated on a weekly basis until, eventually, a winner is chosen. Although the judges determine who reaches the final round of twelve, it is the viewers who determine the next American Idol.

American Idol has proven to be very profitable. 19 Entertainment has earned profits exceeding $100 million dollars; FOX TV is winning the key demographic audience (18-49); many performers, such as Kelly Clarkson, Carrie Underwood, Clay Aiken, Chris Daughtry, and Taylor Hicks have sold millions of albums; and the American public has been treated to great singing performances. However, unless we discuss the shameful self-serving attitude that benefits 19 Entertainment, none of this has anything to do with self-shaming. The self-shaming aspect of *American Idol* is revealed in the early auditions, where numerous people who clearly have no singing talent whatsoever subject themselves to public humiliation via an embarrassing performance on national television. And the growing culture of shamelessness loves this aspect of *Idol*. In fact, one of the primary reasons for the success of *American Idol* is the large viewing ratings for the early rounds, before the "good" singers take center stage.

I must admit, I am one of those people who usually enjoy the early rounds of *American Idol* more than the final elimination rounds. As with millions of viewers, I find it entertaining to listen to Simon humiliate individuals who clearly have no singing ability. And, like many of you, I often wondered, why would people purposely place themselves in a situation to be embarrassed? Certainly someone has told these people they cannot sing, haven't they?! Every year, a number of contestants get blasted by the judges. Usually it is Simon Cowell leading the way. Among Simon's comments, "That was the worse performance I have ever heard" and "I don't know what that was." Simon asked suggested to one male singer, "I don't mean this disrespectfully...shave you're your beard and wear a dress." On another occasion, Simon commented to his fellow judges, Paula and Randy, "We're going to need a bigger a stage" after they told an obese woman that she was going (qualified) to Hollywood.

Of course this is part of the reason why *American Idol* is so popular. The pre-judges are obviously aware how pathetic many of the contestants are but they allow them to advance and sing in front of Randy, Paula, and Simon anyway. They do this because the potential flare-ups between the judges and the shamed "singers" are great for ratings. Thus, it is understandable why the show allows some very bad singers to advance so that they may audition in front of the three judges, but, again, why would any individuals want to place themselves in the situation to be humiliated in front of 35-40 million viewers?

The explanation as to why people will voluntarily self-shame themselves has already been revealed in this chapter. They do it for fame. A person's willingness to humiliate and degrade oneself in front of a large audience appears to actually increase popularity. As Homer Simpson questions in the "Dancin' Homer" episode, "I wonder why stories of degradation and humiliation make you more popular?" Moe, Homer's bartender friend responds, "I don't know. They just do." Indeed, in the rising culture of shamelessness, one's willingness to self-shame often leads to increased popularity. This premise is supported by the thesis that many people wish to be famous.

We all want our "15 minutes of fame," (a phrase coined by Andy Warhol) and remember, the younger generation finds it "most important" to be famous. And, because most of us realize that only a few people are capable of making a living as a singer, there comes the realization that anyone is capable of looking like a fool while trying out for a singing contest. What remains unanswered, to this point, is how did *American Idol* become a medium for someone to seek fame from a singing show by some means other than singing talent? The answer is William Hung, a would-be American Idol who tried out for the show in season three (2004). The first two seasons of *American Idol* were nearly completely limited to airing auditions of "good" singers. This concept disappeared with Hung's appearance.

William Hung sang a rendition of Ricky Martin's "She Bangs" so awful (words fail to describe how terrible he was) that the judges were in shock. His attempts to dance like Martin were, to put it kindly, lousy. The judges thought perhaps Hung was putting them on. At the conclusion of his 90-second audition, Simon quipped, "You can't sing, you can't dance, so what do you want me to say?" Sadly, Hung actually tried his best and thought his performance was acceptable. Why didn't his friends and family warn him? Surely, *anyone* who heard him sing before his tryout for *American Idol* should have warned him not to go through with it; after all, he was definitely going to embarrass himself. "Friends don't let friends sing in public when they cannot even sing in private" should be the motto employed here. Instead, Hung became the poster boy for all self-shamers. He should be one of the first inductees into the Self-shaming Hall of Fame. (Perhaps, I will create a "Self-shaming Hall of Fame" at a future date!) Hung was the butt of jokes from comedians for weeks. *Saturday Night Live* lampooned him. Hung had his 15 minutes of fame, but not how he had imagined.

It would have been reasonable to assume that Hung would simply disappear from the American popular culture consciousness. Curiously, something quite unusual followed Hung's very public humiliation, Americans felt sorry for him. Some even thought the judges were too cruel. There were even a few far-fetched claims of racism. Meaning that, Hung was shamed just because he is Asian. This was an absurd assertion as Hung was just a lousy singer! Regardless of the fact that he tried out for a singing talent show and he could not sing, Hung's popular expanded. He started receiving emails from supportive "fans." His video audition hit the Internet and turned him into a Web cult hero.

The mainstream media became aware of his growing popularity and before long he was appearing on talk shows. He was a "lovable loser." Or, in this case, a "lovable self-shamer." In September 2004, Hung threw out a first pitch at a Los Angeles Dodgers baseball game. And most shocking of all, Hung was offered a record deal from Koch Entertainment. His first album, "Inspiration" includes Ricky Martin's "She Bangs" and "Shake Your Bon Bon" and reached as high as #34 in the charts. His next two albums—yes two!—never reached the charts. He has sold nearly 300,000 total units. Today, Hung enjoys his own website and his merchandise can be found on eBay.

Although William Hung's story is interesting in its own right, the most relevant point for a discussion on self-shaming is that his pitiful performance has paved the way for other self-shamers to audition for *American Idol*. The viewing audience seems to love this. And as a result, *Idol* has increased its focus on self-shamers in the opening round. This has led to two nearly equal focal points for the show, contestants with great voices and/or great life storylines and contestants that think they can sing, who when they are dismissed by the judges blow-up on camera. Acting like an idiot because the judges have shamed them increases the camera time of self-shamers and, correspondingly, extends their 15 minutes of fame. This is a clear reflection of the growing culture of shamelessness.

Other contestants have enjoyed relative fame as a result of their self-shaming willingness to pretend to sing in order to get on TV. In 2007, Kenneth Briggs and Jonathan Jayne became mini-celebrities after being shamed on *American Idol*. Simon Cowell referred to Briggs as a "bush baby" at the conclusion of his audition (Keveney, 2007). Both Briggs and Jayne had absolutely no singing ability, acted as though they were shocked when the judges told them so, berated the judges on camera after they left the judging area, and then received sympathy from a public sucked into believing their performances to be genuine. This pattern has become the format to fame for all Idol contestants that cannot actually sing.

Interestingly, *American Idol* shamelessly took advantage of the popularity that Briggs and Jayne garnered by inviting the two contestants to the 2007 finale show. In 2006, *Idol* added to its finale show a number of awards called the "Golden Idol Awards." Among the categories of awards is the "Best Buddies." American Idol awarded Briggs and Jayne this award. The two buddies appeared with Idol host, Ryan Seacrest, on stage to receive their trophies. Despite the fact that Simon Cowell had mocked him, Briggs actually thanked Simon for making him a star. There's nothing shameful about the story so far, you may be saying to yourself, but I have yet to mention the shameless self-promotion of *Idol*. Seacrest turned everyone's attention to the giant screen on stage where a photo of an actual bush baby was shown. (For those unfamiliar, a bush baby is the name given to a small nocturnal monkey characterized by round eyes and large ears. Briggs is small with distinctive round eyes.) Seacrest announced that American

Idol had donated a bush baby to the Milwaukee County Zoo in "honor" of Briggs. The *Idol* host also informed the audience that the bush baby's name is on record as "Simon." By shamelessly participating in American Idol's 2nd annual "Golden Idol Awards," Briggs and Jayne accomplished extending their undeserving 15 minutes of fame.

American Idol contestants have found another way to increase their 15 minutes of fame by creating their own websites. Ideally, they will have something to promote on their sites. Remembering the earlier discussion on the "sex sells" philosophy, what better way to capitalize on an otherwise short-lived moment of fame than "mysteriously" having provocative photos somehow appear online? Such was the case for at least two attractive female contestants in 2007, Antonella Barba and Shyamali Malakar. Interestingly, Shyamali was eliminated in the semi-final round but she has been able to stay near the limelight because her brother is the much-talked about Sanjaya Malakar (see chapter 3).

The idea that all people want their "15 minutes of fame" and are willing to self-shame, on television no less, helps to explain why contestants voluntarily appear on such trash TV shows as *The Jerry Springer Show* and *The Maury Show*. These "reality" TV shows take shameless pride in revealing embarrassing and humiliating situations that everyday people find themselves in. If your significant other informs you that he or she has something important to tell you but only wants to do it on the Springer or Maury show this should be a warning. Don't go! People are set up for shame on these shows. The uncomplicated plot lines generally follow some sort of script wherein someone is guaranteed to be shamed. For example, a woman announces that she is pregnant, but her boyfriend/husband is not the father. And it might be one of the several other men who is the father. So let's conduct paternity tests right here, right now, on the air. Won't that be fun?! Again, if someone close to you asks you to join her on the Maury Show, don't go! And yet, people go anyway. They go because at least that get to be on TV. Clearly, the culture of shamelessness has found its lowest common denominator with those who embrace the Springer and Maury attitude of life.

Cyberspace: The Ability to Create an Instant Celebrity

As demonstrated by the hoopla surrounding *American Idol* contestant William Hung, there are elements in cyberspace that possess the capability to propel one's status. And with increased status comes increased self-esteem. Not surprisingly, people seeking to increase their social status and expand their identity to a larger circle of acquaintances will take advantage of cyberspace options. Among the primary cyberspace tools used to propel status are Facebook, MySpace, and YouTube (although YouTube has a broader user-base than young people who seek to quantify their friendships on Facebook and MySpace).

Long gone are the days when people marveled at AOL's Instant Messenger which allowed people simultaneously online the ability to carry "conversations" with one another. Today, sites like MySpace and Facebook enable users to create and design personal web pages which they can customize in any manner they choose, including posting photos, poems, thoughts and dreams, or rants about political idealism. For many young people, the sound of an alarm wakes them to a day that begins with a check of email, the weather, sports, and then a visit to their MySpace or Facebook account. And all this is done from the comfort of home.

Facebook

Facebook is a sort of online social mixer meeting place for young people. Facebook users create personal profiles posting their bios and providing links to photos, achievements, buddy lists, and so forth. Facebook allows users to keep up with what their friends (and enemies) are up to, who they are dating, what shows they are watching on TV, what movies they have seen, all without the inconvenience of actually being there with them.

Facebook is not one big site in cyberspace. Instead, it's made up of lots of separate networks based around things like schools, companies, and regions. In this regard, Facebook allows for people who live and/or work closely with one another a chance to become even closer. This reality helps to explain Facebook's mantra: "Facebook is a social utility that connects you with the people around you." Because membership is limited to specific networks, Facebook affords greater privacy controls; and privacy issues are of great concern, especially for parents of children who have web pages.

Although anyone can sign up now, Facebook was originally created (in 2004) as a social networking site for college students. Using a college email account, a student can set up a homepage through his or her college's network. Once the account is set up the student can view all the other pages on the network. Most college students use Facebook to post photos of themselves, friends, and family members; discuss course work and their professors; and to obtain information on upcoming events. College administrators see the value of Facebook as a good method to promote events instead of the traditional posting of fliers around campus that most students ignore. In more extreme cases, such as campus tragedies, Facebook is a place where memorials are set up. Students may post messages of remembrance on the page of a deceased friend.

As a social mixer network, the primary purpose of Facebook is to share information with friends, learn about your friends, and search for new friends within your network. The term "friend" is important with Facebook. Subscribers to Facebook ask other people to be their friends. Once you are "accepted" as a friend you can view personal pages and share information. People who are your friends can share information by writing on your "wall." Many users attempt to secure as many friends as possible. This is a self-esteem enhancement ploy. For many, having a large number of Facebook friends is a sign of popularity and thus their self-esteem is enhanced. In some cases, Facebook not only *introduces* users to friends; it helps to create friendships that develop into romances. In this regard, Facebook is replacing online dating services.

Facebook can also be used to help people decide which college they would like to attend. Potential students can search the network, make friends, and ask questions about the school experience at specific colleges. A number of athletes use Facebook by adding members of a prospective sport's team as their "friends." The student can ask players about the coach and types of practices conducted. In the same manner, potential students can also check into the school's band, intramural activities, the political climate, and so on.

Despite the privacy built-in within the Facebook network, there remain a number of potential negative aspects. For one, users post a great deal of personal information about themselves that can potentially be used against them. For example, if someone posts their schedule on their home page others know when they are in class and not at home—leaving the home vulnerable to burglary. Of greater concern, a predator may wait for someone to come home when he or she will be alone. The predator can find out this information by simply looking at someone's home page.

A great deal of "shaming" also occurs on Facebook pages. In some cases negative comments or shameful photos are posted. And, as per the theme of this chapter, a number of people self-shame by posting "questionable" photos, such as drunk shaming photos. (Note: Drunk shamings will be discussed in detail in chapter 5.)

MySpace

Shaming is more common on MySpace because of the greater number of people who have home pages here than on Facebook. Although there are significant similarities between MySpace and Facebook (e.g., both are primarily social meeting sites), unlike Facebook, a MySpace account can be created using any valid email address, not just a college email address. This helps to explain why MySpace is far more popular than Facebook—it is estimated that MySpace has over 22.5 million registered users (Stone, 2006). It should be noted that the number of registered MySpace and Facebook users continues to increase.

MySpace allows people the opportunity to personalize their profiles in much more detail than Facebook. They can use vivid colors, add music videos, and customize their home pages. But again, the primary purposes of MySpace are similar to Facebook. For example, like Facebook, establishing a website of potential social connections is the goal of MySpace. This idea is illustrated by the MySpace tagline of: "A place for friends." Like Facebook, MySpace provides a "friend request" option. Users ask others to "be my friend" which grants them full access to their web page. Once associates are established, friends can write on the "walls" of other friends as a means of sharing information. It is important to note that users have the option of setting their page on "private" so that no one but their "real" friends and family members are able to see.

MySpace is popular with a wide variety of groups and organizations that hope to promote themselves. Like-minded people who hope to solve a particular problem (e.g., global warming) can use MySpace as a tool to organize others to rallies. Musicians, in particular, take advantage of the MySpace friends list. They sign people up as friends and then send out messages about upcoming scheduled gigs and CD releases. In fact, MySpace originated as a site for musicians. MySpace creator Tom Anderson, a would-be rock star, tried in vain to propel his music career and his band Swank. Anderson believed that he had an audience for his music but he just did not have the avenue to present his music to them. He imagined that the "six degrees of separation" concept could be applied to musicians seeking to find their own audience. The "six degrees of separation" theory was first proposed in 1929 by the Hungarian writer Frigyes Karinthy in a short story called "Chains" (Stephens, 2004). (Stanley Milgram later developed this theory further with his "small world" experiments. Milgram's experiments led to the popular expression, "It's a small world" when people learn of previously unknown connections.) The theory holds that anyone on the planet can be connected to any other person on the planet through a chain of acquaintances that has no more than five intermediaries. In the movie industry, this theory has been applied to actor Kevin Bacon; that is, everyone in Hollywood is connected to Bacon by no more than five intermediaries. According to Todd Stephens (2004), Bacon has an average separation of 2.946 for all the 645,957 registered actors. Presently, there are a wide variety of applications of this "six degrees" theory, including one by MySpace founder Tom Anderson and his desire to create a chain linked by musicians.

The key, Anderson reasoned, was to get the music played to a prospective audience. In 2003, Anderson launched MySpace to give musicians free Web sites on which to post their songs. This also allowed fans the opportunity to build their own websites to spread the word about their favorite new bands. Anderson claims that over 350,000 mostly unsigned bands have made their music available on the website. In 2006, Intermix, the parent company of MySpace.com was purchased by Rupert Murdoch's News Corp for $580 million (Stone, 2006). Musicians worried that the corporate-sponsored MySpace would not be the same, but News Corp pledged to maintain the spirit of "creative anarchy" that has been the trademark of MySpace.

With greater freedom comes greater risk. The MySpace network is not as secure as the Facebook networks. Consequently, there is a greater risk of younger people getting into trouble as they may post photos of themselves that attract online pedophiles. The provocative profiles and photos that some young children have created have led to a number of potential pedophile and child pornography issues. For example, in May 2007 Attorneys General from eight states asked MySpace.com to turn over the names of registered sex offenders who use the network. These top state officials also asked MySpace to describe the methods it has taken to warn users about sex offenders and remove their profiles from the social networking site.

MySpace is an attractive cyber tool for pedophiles because many youngsters post seemingly innocent photos online that tantalize sex perverts. For example, many young girls post photos of themselves in their bathing suits from a family vacation, thinking that only their friends and people from school will be interested in looking at them. These users may be unaware of the fact that one's profile is automatically set to "public" unless it is changed by the user to "private." People may also use MySpace to slam other people in a highly negative fashion. And these hurtful words and misinformation may cause harm to one's emotional well-being and sense of self.

YouTube

YouTube is a website distinct from Facebook and MySpace. Although it can be used as a place to meet new people, like Facebook and MySpace, the primary purpose of YouTube is to post and view videos. On YouTube, people can watch a wide variety of videos, comment on them, and rate them. The idea that nearly any type of video can be found on YouTube was popularized by the comic strip "Close to Home" (5/15/07). In this cartoon a doctor and nurse are shown at the bedside of a patient. The doctor tells the patient, "Great news, Mrs. Janoski! We put a video of your tummy-tuck surgery on YouTube, and it's currently ranked second!"

The videos displayed on YouTube are not supposed to be copyrighted. For example, entire TV show episodes are not supposed to be posted on YouTube. Generally, copyrighted materials are quickly removed from the site. Obviously, if the videos posted are not copyrighted, they come from ordinary people who create short films and want to show the world their creations. As a result, anyone can post a video on any topic matter for the entire cyber world to view. The YouTube motto says it all: "YouTube, Broadcast Yourself."

Although a number of YouTube videos are available to anyone who surfs the net, YouTube does allow people to create accounts. When signing up for an account people are given options in the "Account Type" questionnaire. The options are: "standard," "director," "musician," "comedian," or "guru." Account members are privy to millions of videos and are allowed to upload their own videos. Clearly, with millions of videos available to watch, people surfing this site have lots of time on their hands. However, cyber surfers will find a large number of interesting and funny videos. On the other hand, users will also find a large number of shaming videos. Many of these involve self-shaming. Explanations as to why people would post self-shaming videos on YouTube are the same as those given for any type of self-shaming, including an attempt to gain 15 minutes of fame.

A classic example of a self-shaming video occurred in 2005 when Gary Brolsma of Saddle Brook, N.J., enjoyed his 15 minutes of fame after he uploaded a video of himself singing a Romanian pop song ("Dragostea Din Tei" which translates to "Love From the Linden Trees") while bobbing along in what he calls the "Numa, Numa, Dance." Years ago, Brolsma's humiliating lack of ability to sing or dance would have been kept private, but in the culture of shamelessness people are willing to share their most embarrassing moments with strangers. As it turned out, millions of people viewed his video, creating a mild stir in cyberspace. As a result of this, Brolsma became a web cult hero. He gained celebrity status because of an embarrassing video that he posted. His self-shame led to fame.

Following a brief independent run (it was founded in February 2005); YouTube was purchased by Google Inc in 2006 for $1.65 billion in a stock-for-stock transaction. YouTube continued to operate independently after the acquisition in an effort to preserve its successful brand name and passionately loyal viewing audience. Clearly YouTube has stumbled across the collective conscience of

Americans as its viewers continue to increase in number. It helps that YouTube also enjoys a broad range of viewers, as the young and old and all those in between are attracted to the wide variety of videos of available on YouTube. People who post clever or unusual videos on YouTube have the potential of becoming instant stars, or at the very least, claim their fifteen minutes of fame.

However, the popularity of YouTube does not come without a cost. The fact that any type of video can be posted (at least temporarily) allows for innumerable shaming opportunities—self-shaming or otherwise.

Many people are learning a tough lesson, the photos and short videos that appear on such online sites as Facebook, MySpace, and YouTube that represent youthful indiscretions may actually come back to haunt them when they look for work. Employers are increasingly searching the net in search of any information on potential employees. Everyone needs to heed this warning: Never post anything online that you are not willing to post on your front door or resume. Inevitably, it may come back to haunt you. In short, cyberspace has the potential to shamelessly boost notoriety, but it also has the power to bring someone down in a shameful fashion.

Unhealthy Self-shaming

It has been argued throughout this book that there is a growing culture of shamelessness in the United States and that there is a corresponding escalation in the attempt to curb behaviors once defined as shameful by means of formal and informal degradation (shaming) ceremonies. Proponents of shaming ceremonies are attempting to keep intact certain moral codes of ethical behavior. They want violators, that is, perpetrators of shameful behaviors, to experience and feel shame. Shaming is meant to point out the flaws that people possess and ideally, stimulate them to act more appropriately. When people feel shame they have their self-esteem compromised. Shamed individuals may express their negative sense of self by such statements as, "I'm a failure," "Nobody could possibly love me," and "I am not a good person." Because of this, it is relatively understandable why a sizeable percentage of educators and parents encourage activities that will lead to positive self-esteem, especially for young people. An elevated sense of self, it is reasoned, is better than low self-esteem.

Low self-esteem generally leads to negative feelings of self and when these negative feelings become internalized the individual is at risk of committing a number of unhealthy behaviors, including negative acts as a result of self-hatred, eating disorders (e.g., bulimia and anorexia), and self-mutilations.

Self-hatred: The Perceived Flawed Self

Internalized negative feelings of self may lead to an extreme form of low self-esteem; namely, self-hatred. Self-hatred, or self-loathing, refers to a feeling of intense dislike for oneself or one's own actions. As Gilligan (1996) explains, "To be overwhelmed by shame and humiliation is to experience the destruction of self-esteem; and without a certain minimal amount of self-esteem, the self collapses and the soul dies" (p.48). Those who lack a minimal amount of self-

esteem are ripe for self-hatred. Furthermore, individuals who suffer from prolonged self-hatred risk developing an inferiority complex. For as Gilligan (1996)
states, "nothing is more shameful than to feel ashamed."

When people acknowledge self-shame they have also admitted to themselves that they are flawed. Possessing an image of one's self as being heavily
flawed, due to actions or circumstances, is a key ingredient to self-hatred. Expressing such concerns as "I am no good" or "I am unworthy" are manifesta-
tions of self-hatred.

There are people who repress their shameful feelings and feel guilty about
doing so. Generally speaking, these people will have problems trusting others
and as a result, they limit their contact with others. Because people need interactions with others, this separation anxiety further fuels self-hatred. It is reasoned
that people who suffer from self-hatred lack loving relationships with others.
And people without love in their life risk an ever-increasing sense of self-hatred.
Gilligan (1996) explains, "A joyless life is a synonym for hell. A man who does
not love and cannot love, is, in effect, condemned to hell. His entire environment, from which—without love—he is cut off, is without enjoyment for him,
and thus the world he 'lives' in is a source of emptiness and emotional suffoca-
tion for him. Both the world and the self are experienced and perceived emo-
tionally as being dead, inanimate, without a soul—without feelings" (p.52).

Self-hatred may manifest itself in a variety of ways. For example, self-
haters may have difficulty taking care of their own needs, or may choose to ignore addressing their needs; they may abuse others (taking out their own frustrations on others); they may suffer from depression (hopelessness) and/or rage
(anger); may engage in dangerous addictions and other compulsions; and commit self-abuse. Self-abuse includes eating disorders and self-mutilations.

Eating Disorders

A number of people display their self-hatred via an eating disorder. They
have developed such a negative sense of self that when they look in a mirror the
reflective self is perceived negatively. For example, there are people who are
thin—by any medical definition applied—and yet, they see themselves as overweight and engage in harmful dieting behaviors. On the other hand, some people
eat excessively (compulsive over-eating) because of their negative sense of self.
Either way, these people are engaging in an unhealthy form of self-shaming.

As many as eight million Americans suffer from serious and sometimes
life-threatening eating disorders. An eating disorder involves an abnormal obsession with food and one's weight that harms a person's well-being. Although
it is fairly common for all of us to be somewhat concerned by our weight and
food consumption, people with an eating disorder go to extremes to attain an
"ideal" sense of self. It is more common for women to suffer from eating disorders than men (it is estimated that ninety percent of Americans with eating disorders are women). The primary reason for this is the pressure placed on women
to look a certain way: thin and feminine. In an attempt to reach an "ideal"
weight, women often go on diets, many of which are unhealthy. In fact, some
people are so fixated by fad diets they engage in a behavior known as "disor-

dered eating"—the obsession with consuming foods that they deem "right" for them based on current diet rages (e.g., high protein diets or low carb diets).

Further, it is more common for an adolescent than an older adult to suffer from an eating disorder. Eating disorders are often accompanied by mood disorders, severe mental depression, obsessive-compulsive disorder, or bipolar disorder, and may lead to death, starvation, cardiac arrest, or suicide.

The two most common types of eating disorders, anorexia nervosa and bulimia, involve people who are attempting to keep their weight down and are obsessed with being thin.

Anorexia nervosa is characterized by self-starvation; that is, people who intentionally starve themselves in order to avoid gaining weight. Anorexia is an eating disorder, which usually begins with adolescents around the time of puberty. Anorexics are so obsessed with being thin that they count every calorie they intake or calculate how much fat is in their food. Anorexics have such a negative sense of self that they always think they are overweight even while others tell them they are too thin. They may take diet pills, laxatives, or water pills in an attempt to lose weight (American Academy of Family Physicians, 2006). Anorexics are often so thin, they look sick. And being too thin may result in a host of unhealthy consequences including, stomach problems; heart problems (e.g., abnormally slow heart rate and low blood pressure); osteoporosis (reduction of bone density, which results in dry, brittle bones); irregular periods or no periods; dry and scaly skin; severe dehydration (which can result in kidney failure); fainting, fatigue, and overall weakness; dry hair and hair loss; and the growth of a downy layer of fine hair (called lanugo) all over the body, including the face.

People with bulimia nervosa consume large amounts of food (known as binging), and then rid their bodies of the excessive amount of food by throwing up (known as purging). Thus the expression, "Binge and Purge" is applied to bulimics. In order to "purge" their food, bulimics often place one of the own fingers down their throats to force themselves to vomit. Bulimics are secretive about their self-shaming behavior. They may eat a big meal with friends or family members and then excuse themselves to go to the bathroom; where they vomit. Bulimics may experience weight gains and weight loses as they go from "binge and purge" cycle to the next. They often misuse laxatives, diet pills, and diuretics (water pills) in an attempt to maintain their conception of an ideal body weight. Binging and purging cycles may be stimulated by a variety of emotions including depression, boredom, or anger. Bulimics are often characterized as having a hard time dealing with and controlling impulses, stress, and anxieties (U.S. Department of Health and Human Services, 2007).

As with anorexics, bulimics typically begin their unhealthy behaviors during adolescence. Anorexics and bulimics are usually so ashamed of their self-destructive behaviors that they not only hide their shame, they do not seek help from others. Early diagnosis and treatment for people with eating disorders is important for successful recovery. Additionally, the longer the unhealthy eating behaviors continue, the more difficult it is to overcome the disorder and its negative effects on the body. In some cases, hospitalization is required (U.S. Department of Health and Human Services, 2007). Helping anorexics and bulimics to come and see themselves in a more positive light (beyond their weight) is something friends and family members can do to help them overcome their self-destructive behaviors.

As previously described, people with eating disorders risk an array of unhealthy consequences if they do not learn to accept themselves for who they are and change their destructive behaviors. Thankfully, eating disorders, as with nearly all behaviors, are learned and freely engaged in. Thus, because unhealthy eating decisions are choices, these behaviors can be modified. It takes self-willingness; assistance from friends and family; and, in many cases, professional treatment from medical doctors, health professionals, and dietitians.

Self-mutilations

A self-mutilation involves a person deliberately inflicting injury upon his or her own body. A self-mutilation, or self-injury, is a symptom of a borderline personality disorder and is sometimes associated with mental illness and nearly always with low self-esteem. Self-mutilation is not akin to an attempt at suicide as the person who self-injures is not trying to end his life but is instead attempting to cope with social anxieties in his life. The self-multilator merely wishes to injure or disfigure herself. In essence, people who self-mutilate are mutilating their self-esteem. The severity of the self-mutiliation reflects the level of self-loathing the individual feels toward the self.

There is some debate over whether multiple piercings is an example of a self-mulititaion, as "piercers" are sometimes equated with "cutters" because both categories of people have altered (multilated) their bodies. At one time, people who inked their bodies with multiple tattoos were considered self-multiliators. However, with the large percentage of people in the United States that currently have tattoos, it is highly unlikely most consider themselves self-mutilators. As for "piercers" who have multiple visible piercings, especially facial peiercings, the jury is out. Piercers do not pierce themselves multiple times for aesthetics purposes as they are seldom considered more attractive; instead, they do so as a means to express their individuality or draw attention to themselves.

There are commonly identified forms of self-injury, including punching, hitting, and scratching; choking; self-biting; picking at wounds or blemishes; burning; stabbling the self; and ingesting dangerous chemicals and/or posions. Perhaps the most commonly recongnized form of self-mutilation involves "cutting." Cutting involves making shallow cuts to the skin of the arms or legs. People who do this for a prolonged period of time are known as "cutters." Cutters are overwhelmingly adolescents and their self-shaming behavior is linked to interpersonal stress caused by such variables as feeling socially isolated; abandoment; neglect; or being a victim of physical, mental, or sexual abuse. Unlike piecers, cutters attempt to hide their self-injury as they generally prefer to avoid unwanted attention. They also display the classic sympton of embarassment with their sense of self-shame.

Living In a Growing Culture of Shamelessness and Being Proud of It!

Self-shaming further fuels the culture of shamelessness. When people are willing to engage in behaviors previously labeled as shameful, there is, seemingly, little hope for those who cling to past notions of morality. And yet, once again we can find a counterbalance to the growing incidence and influence of self-shaming on society; this time, in the form of national pride. According to survey data results released by the National Opinion Research Center at the University of Chicago in 2006, Americans were ranked number one (out of 34 countries) in national pride. People were asked to rate how proud of their countries they were in 10 areas: political influence, social security, the way their democracy works, economic success, science and technology, sports, arts and literature, military, history, and fair treatment of all groups in society (*The Post-Standard*, 6/28/06). Venezuela came in a close second; Ireland came in third and was followed by South Africa and Australia, respectively.

Interestingly, admitting to being proud is considered shameful in some societies because it is, after all, one of the seven "deadly sins." Thus, while it could be argued that pride is an important component of American culture, and thus a counterforce to the growing culture of shamelessness, people from other cultures might argue that American pride is simply another example of shamelessness.

Americans tend to value pride—which may be defined as a high or inordinate opinion of one's own importance, merit, or superiority—because it is a mechanism designed to increase self-esteem. Taking pleasure or satisfaction in something, someone, or one's self is to be proud. And despite the fact that some cultures, such as those found in the Asian societies of Japan, Taiwan, and Korea, view boastful behaviors as both bad luck and poor manners, pride is viewed in American society as a form of commitment to the greater community. And ties that bind a society are not considered to be shameful. Rather, they are viewed as proper and acceptable.

Chapter 5

Drunk Shamings: An Old College Tradition Meets Modern Technology

"The Person Who Shames First, Risks Being Shamed Back Double"— Tim Delaney (American social thinker)

Jimbo Hahn wakes up one Saturday morning feeling a little groggy and with a splitting headache. He is quite disoriented when he firsts awakes and finds it difficult to get up out of bed. Only after he rises does Jimbo discover that he did not sleep in his own bed last night. Not only that, but Jimbo realizes he fell asleep on the floor of a friend's apartment. He struggles to recall the previous evening's events. Jimbo is a college freshman.

Other partygoers from the night before also begin to rise as they hear Jimbo's commotion. As Jimbo asks, "What did I do last night?" his friends laugh. After being told there was no juice or aspirin in the house, Jimbo is sent to the local convenience store. His friends laugh loudly as he heads out the door. Jimbo is unsure why. At the local market, shoppers look at Jimbo and also laugh. Again, he is unsure why. The cashier rings up his purchases and asks, "Did you look in the mirror before you came here?" Jimbo gives the cashier a polite, "No, I didn't. Why do you ask?" "No reason," replies the cashier as she laughs.

As he walks back to his friend's apartment, Jimbo takes a peek of himself in the mirror of a parked car. Jimbo is shocked by his appearance. His face is covered with obscene words and drawings drawn with a permanent black marker. Jimbo is a "victim" of a drunk shaming. Initially, Jimbo is quite embarrassed; especially after he remembers all the strangers he saw at the convenience store. When Jimbo returns to the site of the shaming his friends are waiting for him. They quickly figure out that Jimbo has seen the drawings on his face, after having gone to the store. Despite his obvious displeasure of having been victimized by a drunk shaming, Jimbo's friends laugh hysterically at his predicament. Jimbo's embarrassment is their entertainment. Shortly thereafter, Jimbo lightens up and realizes that his own drunken behavior the night before is the cause of his shaming. Having been punk'd by a drunk shaming, Jimbo laughs at his own folly. However, he vows "revenge" against his friends, saying, "One of these days, I will shame you twice back."

Such is the nature of a drunk shaming. A person drinks too much, passes out on a friend's couch or on the floor, and becomes the object of others' creative and artistic expression of: "You had it coming, pal!" For many young people, a drunk shaming represents a rite of passage; especially for college students recently out of high school.

Rites of Passage

There are many rites of passages (traditions) that young adults participate in while attending college. For most college students, this is their first time away from home and being on their own, or least without constant parental supervision. Among the more lasting rites of passage of young adults attempting to "find themselves" is the consumption of alcohol, often in excessive form (Lederman and Stewart, 2005; Walters and Baer, 2006). Walters and Baer (2006) cite surveys that show young adults tend to increase their drinking dramatically upon entrance into college. Drinking on college campuses is hardly a recent occurrence. In fact, in the early 1700s, Harvard University sold beer and wine in the college dining halls as well as the butteries in an attempt to keep students from drinking brandy, rum and other distilled spirituous liquors (Wechsler and Wuethrich, 2002). There were numerous reported "eruptions of alcohol-fueled rowdiness on college campuses" throughout the nineteenth century (Wechsler and Wuethrich, 2002:27). Drinking rowdiness among college students continued to increase throughout the twentieth century. On many college campuses, binge drinking has become a standard rite of passage for students. Binge drinking is defined as five or more drinks on one occasion for males and four or more for females (Weitzman, Nelson, and Wechsler, 2003; Lederman and Stewart, 2005). Other rites of passage involving alcohol on college campuses include such activities as "beer pong" and "funneling" tournaments; playing quarters; dollar pitcher nights at bars; and drinking jell-o shots. Today, nearly one-fourth of all college students binge drink more than once a week (Wechsler and Wuethrich, 2002). People who drink to excess not only risk harm to their own personal safety and health, but that of others as well. As demonstrated in this chapter's introductory story, some people drink so much they actually forget many details of their day/evening. When they are told of their drunken exploits by their friends and acquaintances, they generally just laugh it off.

Throughout the centuries that college students have been drinking to excess their friends have been known to mock their behavior. They would retell stories and embellish the tales of drunkenness. With the advent of photographic technology, friends began to take photos of each other in various drunken states. These photos may be used for "blackmail" or serve as future funny reminders of out-of-control behavior from one's younger years. Today, technological advancements have afforded people an opportunity to post drunk shaming photos on the Internet. Cell phone photography has made it especially easy to capture drunken behavior while it occurs. In short, people have always mocked their drunken friends, but with modern technology, the mocking, or shaming, can be instantly spread to a much larger viewing audience.

Alcohol Consumption

It is recognized that throughout most of humanity, people have sought ways to alleviate pain and/or heighten pleasure. "No record is to be found which tells the story of man's first use of alcoholic beverages. In all probability he began to use them in prehistoric times. Although alcohol per se was not known in antiquity, fermented and brewed beverages, wines and beers...have been known to practically all peoples from the dawn of history, and doubtless long before" (Patrick, 1952:12). Consuming alcohol is presumed by many to be an effective means of alleviating stress, hurt, and discomfort. In fact, the foremost reason for drinking is most likely to alter one's feeling. For young people, consuming alcohol is a viewed as a "social lubricant" wherein inhibitions are lowered or released. Drinking with peers is a way of strengthening group bonds.

Alcohol has been both condemned and defended. It has been blamed for many societal social problems and interpersonal problems, and praised as an "acceptable" escape from the pressures of everyday life. As Glidden-Tracey (2005) explains, "Every day huge numbers of people use drugs or alcohol for recreation, medication, celebration, stress management, worship, social lubrication, or escape. Although some substance use is considered normal, it is no secret that drug and alcohol consumption can become excessive or compulsive to the point where it disrupts normal human functions" (p.1).

Research has shown that there are many potential harmful effects for those who consume alcohol. "They include drowsiness, slower reaction time, deterioration of motor performance and coordination skills, loss of concentration and memory, and deterioration of intellectual performance. Long-term use of alcohol can cause cirrhosis" (*International Labour Office*, 2003:10). In some cases, alcohol poisoning and death can occur if alcohol is consumed in excess (and in some rare cases, after just one drink). On the other hand, when used in moderation, nearly all people can consume a daily drink of alcohol (e.g., a glass of wine with dinner) without any immediate negative physical or mental health consequences. Almost one-half (44%) of Americans report that they are current drinkers and have consumed at least 12 drinks in the preceding year (Cooney, Kadden, and Steinberg, 2005). Consuming alcohol is a relatively common behavior for Americans. Thus, to no one's surprise, college students are also known to drink alcohol. They are a part of a "culture of alcohol."

Customs with Drinking

Drunken behavior has been the subject of analysis since at least biblical times. *The Holy Bible* itself presents contradictory opinions on the matter of drinking alcohol; specifically, wine. Paul the Apostle's First Epistle to Timothy 3 describes the qualifications of Bishops: A bishop must be sober and of good behavior and his wife must be sober (*The Holy Bible: King James Version*, 2000). Proverbs 20:1 states, "Wine is a mocker, strong drink is raging: and whosoever is deceived thereby is not wise." On the other hand, there are many references in the Bible that acknowledge the positive aspects of drinking: Wine is praised; it rejoices God and men (Judges 9:13); it gladdens the heart of men (Psalms 104:15); it gladdens life (Exodus 10:19); it makes the heart exult (Zechariah 10:7); it cheers the spirits of the depressed (Proverbs 31:6) (McKenzie, 1965). Then again, there are passages in the Bible that stress moderation: "Let your moderation be known unto all men" (Philippians 4:5); Paul tells Timothy, "Drink no longer water, but use a little wine;" and when he wrote to the Ephesians, he states, "And be not drunk with wine, wherein is excess." Drinking in moderation is the rallying cry of most in contemporary society.

Mendelson and Mello state in the Introduction to Alan Lang's *The Encyclopedia of Psychoactive Drugs: Alcohol and Teenage Drinking* (1992) that alcohol use and misuse was associated with the worship of gods and demons during the ancient Greek and Roman eras. "One of the most powerful Greek gods was Dionysus, lord of fruitfulness and god of wine. The Romans adopted Dionysus but changed his name to Bacchus. Festivals and holidays associated with Bacchus celebrated the harvest and the origins of life. Time has blurred the images of the Bacchanalian festival, but the theme of drunkenness as a major part of celebration has survived the pagan gods and remains a familiar part of modern society" (p.13).

The highly centralized monarchy of the ancient Ashanti of West Africa considered drunkenness as a valid defense for all crimes but homicide and cursing the king (Hoebel, 1964). The Ashanti were less forgiving toward the mentally ill. The rationale behind this forgiving attitude toward drunks was exemplified during the reign of King Osai Yao. The king set up an experiment. His men placed a "madman" and a drunk in a house and set it ablaze. The burning madman screamed as he fled the house. The drunk, in oblivious stupor, never fled and was thus cremated. "The conclusion was obvious to Osai Yao. A drunk does not know what is going on. Ergo, drunkenness shall remain as a mitigating plea in defense. Insanity, though it may impair, does not completely paralyze perception. Ergo, there is no validity to the old plea of insanity as a defense. The plea was abolished" (Hoebel, 1964:238).

Early Egyptian carvings reveal that drinking excessively was quite common among Pharaohs and citizens alike. The ancient Indo-Aryan tribes of India had an intoxicating drink called *soma*, which was offered as a libation to their deities. Drinking soma became an integral aspect in their ceremonies. Perhaps the ancient culture most associated with the consumption of alcohol is the Roman Empire. Both men and women would attempt to out-drink the other and drunken orgies are well documented.

Many contemporary college students reenact the ancient "toga" party with Greek roots but Roman consequences. The movie *Animal House* forever immortalized the toga party as an accepted form of behavior for American college students. Beyond the toga party, the "culture of alcohol" on college campuses is common to fraternity and sorority initiations, football tailgating parties, birthday celebrations (especially the twenty-first birthday), "bar crawls," and so on. Throughout the mid- to-late twentieth century the culture of alcohol was intertwined in school customs and social functions. For young students, the culture of alcohol places pressures on them to drink or risk being labeled a "dork" or "nerd." As Lederman and Stewart (2005) explain, "The image of excessive drinking and perpetually inebriated college students is a cliché in the media and contemporary American culture. It often seems as if the popular view of the college student is somehow incomplete without a reference to the 'typical' alcohol-doused, rowdy college party" (p.5).

The culture of alcohol on college campuses is not limited to the students. The entire academic community needs to evaluate its own alcoholic behavior. For faculty, administrators, alumni, and college guests, alcohol is a regular fixture at many social events and gatherings. This culture of alcohol attempts to "normalize" the use of alcohol on college campuses. Of course, the culture of alcohol has a dark side as well. Many college students engage in "dangerous drinking" (a term used to describe those who consume unhealthy quantities of alcohol) and pose a great risk to the college community (Lederman and Stewart, 2005).

Dangerous Drinking Habits

Undergraduate students who engage in dangerous drinking habits do so as a means of fulfilling social interaction needs that are a part of the culture of alcohol. It is estimated that fourteen hundred college students aged eighteen to twenty-four are killed each year as a result of drinking from alcohol-related motor vehicle crashes, other unintentional injuries, and alcohol overdoses (Wechsler and Wuethrich, 2002).

By the twenty-first century there was a noticeable trend unveiling itself on many college campuses across the United States—a crackdown on alcohol use. Many college campuses have banned alcohol at residence halls, fraternities and sororities. As a result, most heavy drinking occurs off-campus. College campuses that are cracking down on alcohol consumption usually turn to intervention programs and education on the harms of drinking. Zero-tolerance policies and strict enforcement of anti-alcohol policies on campus have help contribute to the growing number of reported alcohol violations. For example, alcohol violations on Central New York college campuses increased twenty-five percent in two years. College officials say this increase reflects the crackdown on drinking (Coin, 2005). Many State University of New York (SUNY) schools witnessed double the number of drinking violations reported to college officials from 2002 to 2004. SUNY Oswego, for example, saw a fifty-three percent increase in alcohol violations during this two year period (Coin, 2005). It should be noted that the increase in recorded alcohol violations at schools such as SUNY Oswego may be attributed to the fact that students are now referred to the campus judiciary systems more than they used to be. The SUNY schools also happen to be located in a region (the Northeast) with the highest heavy-drinking rates (Walters and Baer, 2006). The extremely cold winters (which keep people indoors and less physically active) are often cited by students as a contributing cause to their heavy drinking. Cold winters coupled with the perceived rites of passage associated with drinking mass quantities of alcohol are fertile breeding grounds for drunk shamings.

Drunken Comportment

The effects of alcohol on human behavior are subject to great variation. When people drink, some become happy, others depressed; some become outgoing, others withdrawn; some vicious, others pleasant; and some become energetic, while others are more passive. Furthermore, some people can "hold their liquor" and others cannot.

A common belief about the effect of alcohol on behavior is that alcohol automatically reduces inhibitions; that is, drinkers expect alcohol to improve their sociability. Lang (1992) argues "it may be the expectation itself that gives alcohol this property" (p.35). MacAndrew and Edgerton (1969) conducted an extensive and often cited study of alcohol and its impact on human behavior. In their book *Drunken Comportment*, MacAndrew and Edgerton report that the view of alcohol as universally acting as a "releaser of inhibitions" is false. People are not simply under the control of alcohol. Instead, people act as they have been taught to act when drunk. This concept has been illustrated on such early TV shows as *The Honeymooners*, where in one episode, Ralph Kramden and Ed Norton got "drunk" on grape juice.

MacAndrew and Edgerton argue that individuals *learn* that that they should feel less inhibited when drunk and therefore *act* drunk. In other words, one's behavior while "under the influence" of alcohol does not follow a predetermined, biochemically fixed pattern—it follows a learned pattern of behavior.

> Rather than viewing drunken comportment as a function of toxically disinhibited brains operating in impulse-drive bodies, we have recommended that what is fundamentally at issue are the learned relations that exist among men living together in society. More specifically, we have contended that the way people comport themselves when they are drunk is determined not by alcohol's toxic assault upon the seat of moral judgment, conscience, or the like, but by what their society makes of and imparts to them concerning the state of drunkenness (MacAndrew and Edgerton, 1969:165).

MacAndrew and Edgerton (1969) conclude that if we are ever to understand drunken comportment, we must concentrate research on the shared understandings of the nature of drunkenness among groups of people found in society.

The purpose of this chapter is to gain a greater understanding of the drunken comportment among those involved in drunk shamings. It is my contention that drunk shamings represent a learned acceptable form of behavior among young adults (e.g., college students); that it is a part of their comportment. Further, drunk shamings are a normative aspect of the culture of alcohol.

It should be noted that many high school students look forward to college because they have already heard about the culture of alcohol and the normative behaviors associated with being a college student. Thus, many freshmen start their college careers ready, eager, and willing to drink—including binge and dangerous levels of drinking. (In fact, many students enter college having experienced binge and dangerous drinking and have already participated in drunk shamings.) These students are often exposed to an environment and culture that supports the idea that drinking to excess is an acceptable norm. This culture includes the encouragement of increasingly dangerous behaviors. In other words, when someone starts to act a little "crazy" and "out of control" they are encouraged by others to continue their wild ways. Fueled by more alcohol and encouragement, the inhibition of many college students diminishes. As a rule, college students excuse their drunken behavior (the next day) by simply saying, "I was drunk"—assuming that others will view this as a legitimate excuse for nearly any behavior. It also helps drunk persons justify and rationalize their behavior. In most cases, this haphazard apology is acceptable within the culture of alcohol.

Despite the crackdown on alcohol consumption on a growing number of college campuses, the culture of alcohol has made it acceptable among college students to drink to excess (binge), act wild and crazy, and feel little remorse for their behavior. The culture of alcohol among many college students teaches new recruits that acting stupid and drinking themselves into a drunken stupor is acceptable. Subjecting themselves to a quasi-degradation ceremony—the drunk shaming—is taught as an acceptable form of behavior for young adults. Thanks to modern technology, the drunken behavior of people may be captured for posterity and displayed to a wide audience.

Drunk Shamings

As previously mentioned, many younger college students drink, some to excess. People who drink excessively not only risk harm to themselves and others; act foolishly and often look ridiculous; they also risk being victimized by a "drunk shaming." Drunk shamings are an example of an informal degradation ceremony designed to shame and embarrass the victim. Degradation ceremonies represent attempts by others to alter one's identity by means of embarrassment and shame. Degradation ceremonies force the victims to yield to the wishes of others who are in a position of authority.

As described in chapter 2, military court martials are an example of a formal degradation ceremony. In some cases, a court martial may become a public spectacle, such as the case of Pfc. Lynndie R. England, a defendant from the notorious abuses at Abu Ghraib prison. Technology played a major role in this degradation ceremony. Photos of prisoner abuse taken by U.S. reservists on their cell phones and transmitted via the Internet led to the Abu Ghraib incident becoming public and England's eventual conviction. England's military degradation ceremony was preceded by a "drunk shaming." Shortly after the 372nd Unit received its orders to go to Iraq in February 2003, Private England and Private Charles Graner (with whom England was romantically involved) and another soldier had a last party weekend in Virginia Beach. They reportedly drank heavily and when their friend passed out, Private Graner and Private England took turns taking photographs of each other exposing themselves over his head (Zernike, 2005). Taking photos of a drunken friend is becoming increasingly typical with young adults who have access to technology. (One simply needs to do a Google search for a near endless number of examples of drunk shamings.)

Drunk shamings represent a rather unique type of contemporary degradation ceremony. They are unique in that drunk shamings are generally not planned; they are spontaneous degradation ceremonies. In my own research (conducted with the assistance of a former student of mine, Patrick Tanzini) on drunk shamings, it was revealed that ninety-five percent of drunk shamings were not planned. The five percent of planned shamings were in retaliation for previous shaming victimization our respondents indicated. (Note: Our research design will be explained later in this chapter).

People who drink to excess risk many potential bodily harms (e.g., death or injury from a fall or car accident) but they also risk shame and embarrassment as well as a potential blow to their self-identity and self-esteem (to be discussed later in this chapter) via a drunk shaming.

What is a Drunk Shaming?

A drunk shaming occurs when people become too drunk to defend themselves from a private or public shaming. A drunk shaming is an example of a quasi-degradation ceremony because it is conducted informally; usually by close friends and/or family members. Often, the drunk person will have his or her picture taken and sometimes placed on the Internet. Drunk shamings generally entail a four-step process:

Step 1:   A person(s) drinks excessively (in the company of a group of other people) to the point where he or she passes out drunk.
Step 2:   Someone from the group of other people needs to take action. That is, he or she needs to start the drunk shaming process.
Step 3:   Some application of a method(s) of drunk shaming must be conducted.
Step 4:   The drunk shaming is captured for posterity on film or video; which may then be posted online.

As stated in Step 3 of the drunk shaming process, some sort of drunk shaming method must be initiated. And there are a number of drunk shaming methods from which shamers may choose. The most common method of drunk shaming involves drawing (usually with a black permanent marker) on the victim's skin (especially derogatory and obscene messages). This type of drunk shaming was demonstrated in a scene from the movie *Garden State*. The character Andrew Largerman, played by Zach Braff, is on an MRI machine after a night of partying (drinking and taking other drugs) and he has drawings of male genitalia and other obscene things drawn on his body.

Other shaming methods include, putting objects on/near the victim (e.g., clothing, beer bottles, sex toys); exposing the victim by taking his/her clothing off; shaving eyebrows and/or hair; duct taping a shamee to toilets, walls, chairs, beds, and so on; wrapping the shamee in plastic wrap; and rearranging the victim's body into embarrassing positions. In some cases, perpetrators of a drunk shaming may employ shaming techniques known as "antiquing" and "tar and feather." Antiquing and "tar and feather" shamings are combination shamings.

Antiquing is best described by two respondents to a survey conducted by myself and Patrick Tanzini. (Note: This survey design will be discussed later in this chapter.) One of our questions read: "In what manner did you shame the victim(s)?" One respondent stated, "We antiqued them! First we wet their faces with a washcloth and then we threw flour on them. The flour stuck because their faces were damp." Another respondent stated, "Me and about 4 of my friends dampened the face of our buddy who was drunk and passed out. Next, we got baby powder, flour, and powdered sugar and poured it all over him. We antiqued him!"

The "tar and feather" is a variation of the antiquing shaming. Instead of pouring hot tar on the drunk victim, shamers pour a sticky substance (e.g. honey) on the shamee and then dump feathers or stuffing (e.g., from a pillow) on the victim.

Many of the other drunk shaming methods have names as well. For example, using a sharpie marker to draw on someone is known as "marking." Dressing a male shaming victim in women's clothing is known as the "J. Edgar Hoover" and shaving a person completely bald is known as the "Hairless Henderson." Placing items on the drunk person is sometimes called the "tumble" game. When playing "tumbling" perpetrators of drunk shamings take turns placing items on top of the shamee while waiting for the victim to shift his or her body position and wake up. If the drunk person wakes up from the noise he is safe for the rest of the night; but if he remains asleep, he is fair game for continued shaming. Undoubtedly, participants of drunk shamings use a variety of other names for these same acts.

Drunk Shaming Rules

Drunk shamings involve an emergent form of embarrassment opportunity. Any person who drinks excessively is a potential victim of drunk shaming. Although most drunk shamings are administered by friends (seventy-one percent based on our research), complete strangers may also victimize a drunk person (three percent based on our research).

However, as demonstrated by the "tumbling" game, there are rules that are generally adhered to by the shaming community. For example, because drunk shamings are meant to be "good natured" fun, the victim is not to be physically harmed. Drunk shamings are designed to embarrass the victim, not injure the person.

Nearly all drunk shaming participants recognize that the host of a party is not to be shamed. It is a sign of respect to the person for hosting the party. Thus, if the host passes out drunk, the guests should make sure that he or she is safely placed in bed before continuing the party—house guests should not be expected to quit partying just because the host is a lightweight, right?! Closely related to the idea that the host is free from a potential drunk shaming is the concept of "house rules." Everyone understands that whenever social gatherings occur or a game is played that local rules and expectations are to be followed. Generically, this is known as "house rules." For example, the host of the party may state that no drunk shamings are allowed or only certain types of shamings are allowed. The house rules may also include a provision that the host has to approve all drunk shamings. Of course, when young people are involved, the host is most likely to encourage group participation of a drunk shaming because she realizes that people are having fun while conducting a drunk shaming. A perfectly executed drunk shaming may lead to legendary status and, clearly, the host benefits from this label.

Perhaps the most accepted rule of drunk shamings is: if the drunk person is asleep in his or her own bed, they cannot be shamed. This is because he or she was at least conscious enough (or lucky enough) to make it there. However, any person who passes out on your bed—that you have not invited to sleep with you—or on the floor is fair game for a drunk shaming.

Another primary drunk shaming rule involves people who fall asleep with their shoes on. Any drunk that falls asleep with his shoes on is fair game for a drunk shaming. There is a debate in the drunk shaming community as to whether a person who passes out on her bed but with shoes on is fair game for a shaming. After all, she made it to her bed safely, which disavows her from a shaming; but, she passed out with her shoes on.

There is also a rule that involves the presence of the drunk person's significant other. Generally speaking, if someone is about to be victimized by a drunk shaming but his or her significant other is also present; the shamers need permission from the boyfriend or girlfriend. This is yet another reminder for people to choose their significant others wisely! Generally, the significant other will agree to allow the shaming. This is the case because usually the significant other felt embarrassed by the behavior of the soon-to-be shamed person or yielded to peer pressure.

A number of drunk shaming participants inform me that visitors are always fair game for a drunk shaming. The idea behind this rule is tied directly to the expectation that visitors, in general, are always expected to abide by "house rules" and to make every attempt at behaving properly while at someone else's domain. There are occasions where multiple visitors become possible targets for a drunk shaming. The general rule of thumb followed here is that the most annoying guest at the party becomes the primary target of a shaming.

There are drunk shaming rules that involve property; especially the rule that demands: leave people's cars alone. A student told me of a drunk shaming that involved a group of people decorating the car of a drunk person who happened to work for the fire department. The next morning, after the drunk shaming victim awoke from his stupor, he was summoned to work before he could clean off his car. Once he arrived at work he became a victim of a formal shaming from the fire department; that is, he was suspended from work. The Fire Chief did not appreciate the humor of his decorated car that included obscene drawings. Another respondent indicated that she was a part of a group that shamed a drunk person at a house party by placing slices of bologna on the victim's car. Apparently, after removing the bologna slices from the car, circles are left behind from where the bologna has stripped the car's paint off!

As was the case with firefighters, it seems that the profession of the drunk victim is to be considered when deciding how to shame the individual. A number of respondents indicate that if the person holds a professional job shamers are not supposed to use permanent markers on areas of skin typically exposed at work. This leads us to, perhaps, the "Golden Rule" of drunk shamings is, "Don't shame others in ways you wouldn't want to be shamed."

Rules are generally adhered to because they are a part of the degradation ceremony protocol. "Interrelated with self-presentation concerns is our desire to behave in a way which is generally consistent with social rules. The structure of rule-governed behavior is so closely linked with embarrassment that classifications of embarrassing events are often based upon the types of rule violations which give rise to identity-threatening predicaments" (Edelmann, 1987:17). However, just as there are deviants in society, there are those who do not adhere to the shaming rules within the drunk shaming community. In other words, a drunk person who happens to make it to his or her bed and take his or her shoes off may still be subject to a drunk shaming. (Note: Instances of rule violations will be shared later in this chapter where I provide a number of drunk shaming examples.) Further, there are those within the drunk shaming community who flat-out refuse to acknowledge any rules. As one respondent stated, "There are no rules. Any time someone passes out because they are too drunk, they are fair game!"

Drunk Shamings and Technology

There have always been people who have mocked and attempted to shame the drunken behavior of their friends for centuries. College students are among these people. However, with the advent of technology, such as cell phones, dorm rooms with web cams, and so forth, drunk shamings have reached a new level of sophistication. "Drunk shaming is not new; it has been honed to a fine art by legions of young men across the country, perhaps for decades. The Internet has transformed drunk shamings into a public spectacle" (Copeland, 2005:H-1). There are numerous websites (e.g., CollegeHumor.com; BangedUp.com; and MySpace.com) that post drunk shaming photos on the Internet. For example, one photo that appeared on Shamings.Com showed an individual saran-wrapped to his bed with a caption that read, "We luv ya but you know you deserved it!" It should be noted that these websites are so popular that Shamings.com, which started as a spin-off of CollegeHumor.com, claims to have received almost 8 million hits in December 2004 alone. Web watcher ComScore Media Metrix states that the figure is closer to one million (Copeland, 2005). Whether it is one million or eight million, this is just one website (designed to post alcohol-themed content) in one month's time; clearly drunk shamings are a social phenomenon and an aspect of the contemporary culture of alcohol.

Internet technology exerts a great deal of influence in nearly all spheres of life. People use the Internet to search for information, surf various sites of interest, and of course, send emails to their friends and families. Personal websites and blogs are becoming increasingly popular with Internet users. Personal websites generally provide bulletin boards and personal information links (See chapter 4). Blogs are similar to personal journals or diaries but they are posted online for others to read. Advancements in cell phone technology over the past two decades are nearly astronomical. Cell phones have been available for twenty years, but the phones used today are dramatically different from the first, almost primitive variations of cell phones. Today's cell phones not only take pictures and videos and permit text messaging, they allow for streamline video. College students who engage in drunk shaming ceremonies often utilize cell phones to take embarrassing photos of shaming victims. Posting these photos and/or videos online represents the centerpiece of the old college tradition of drunk shaming meeting technology.

It is the use of technology that has propelled drunk shamings into the forefront of popular culture and the culture of alcohol on many college campuses throughout the United States.

Perpetrators, Victims, and Self-shamers: Researching Drunk Shamings

In 2005, I conducted original research (with the help of Patrick Tanzini) on the drunk shaming behaviors of college students at a state university. A "Drunk Shaming" questionnaire consisting of a combination of sixty-three open-ended and closed-ended questions was completed by one hundred twenty-four students. Seventy-three respondents (59%) had been directly involved in a drunk shaming and thirty-seven (30%) respondents were victims of a drunk shaming. Twenty-seven respondents (23%) admitted to self-shaming. Follow-up interviews were conducted with a number of respondents who had participated in drunk shamings.

A number of questions from the drunk shaming questionnaire were designed to ascertain the drinking habits of respondents and the prevalence of the culture of alcohol. Self-reporting is a common method of assessing alcohol consumption. Generally speaking, self-report data on alcohol consumption is deemed accurate (Cooney, et. al., 2005). The vast majority (74.2%) of respondents reported that they drink alcohol "occasionally;" while 16.9 percent reported that they seldom drink and 1.6 percent indicated that they never drink. Only four percent specified that they drink alcohol daily. Just 5.6 percent of respondents claim to have a drinking problem; whereas 24.2 percent reported that they were told they had a drinking problem. This data indicates that a number of students are either in denial about their drinking or have become so accustomed to the culture of alcohol that their problem drinking has been rationalized. The climate of culture experienced by the respondents in our research is also reflected by the responses to the questions that asked about the frequency of drinking by the majority of their friends and whether or not respondents had close friends with a drinking problem. Nearly half (48%) of all respondents reported that they had close friends with a drinking problem and 57.3 percent of respondents indicated that the majority of their friends were moderate drinkers and 16.9 percent of friends were heavy drinkers.

A number of demographic and background questions were also asked, including gender, race/ethnicity, age (17-20, 21-23, 24-28, 29 and over), socialization environment (raised primarily in an urban, suburban, or rural environment), campus residency, frequency of consumption of alcohol, location where most drinking takes place (e.g., at home, a dorm, a bar, or a house party), and friends with a drinking problem. Because of the element of immaturity involved and the fact that females tend to mature at an earlier age than males, it was hypothesized that males are more likely to engage in drunk shamings than females. Immaturity is also often an aspect of age; consequently, we theorized that younger people are more likely to be involved in drunk shamings than older respondents. Specifically, we suspected that the youngest legal age category of respondents are the most likely to be involved in drunk shamings. The demographic question that asks for one's socialization environment is a relatively new concept utilized in research. Delaney and Tanzini (2005) suspected that drunk shamings are a part of the greater culture of alcohol and therefore would be found near equally in all socialization environments. Because of the growing trend to forbid alcohol consumption on college campus dorms, it was also hypothesized that drunk shamings would be more common off-campus (e.g., house parties or a friend's home) than in a dorm. Further, because it is easier to control the environment at a house party or a friend's home than it is in a public place, it was expected that drunk shamings are relatively rare at bars.

Experiencing a Drunk Shaming: "I woke up with a jar of peanut butter, a banana with a condom on it in my hand, and a shovel was on me."

It was an article written by Libby Copeland (2005), which first drew my attention and stimulated my research effort into the phenomenon of drunk shamings. Copeland believes that drunk shamings are a "white" phenomenon. However, because the vast majority (93%) of survey respondents were white it was statistically impossible to determine whether drunk shamings are also predominant with other specific races and/or ethnicities. However, Copeland is not alone in her belief that drunk shamings are a "white thing." Black comedian Dave Chappelle has an interesting racial take on drunk shamings: "You cannot pass out around white people. Every time white dudes pass out around each other, they always do some borderline gay shit when the guy's asleep...'Frank fell asleep so we, like, stuck a carrot in his ass and put shaving cream on his balls'" (from his 2004 *Showtime* comedy special, "For What It's Worth"). Chappelle questions why white people shame their drunk friends; after all, they *are* friends. Chappelle further argues that "a black guy will kill you" when he wakes up and finds that he has been victimized by a drunk shaming. Conversely, white people realize that the rules of passing out at a friend's house leave one open for a shaming.

Copeland (2005) also states that drunk shamings are primarily the purview of the male half of the species. In our research, fifty-one respondents were male and seventy-three were female. Thirty-five percent of the males and twenty-six percent of the females were victims of drunk shamings (See Table 5.1).

Table 5.1
Victim of Drunk Shaming by Sex
In Percent

Sex	Yes	No
Male	35	65
Female	26	74

Furthermore, seventy-six percent of the males and forty-seven percent of the females were perpetrators of drunk shamings (See Table 5.2). As the data from Tables 5.1 and 5.2 indicate, males are more likely to be involved in drunk shamings—both as victims and perpetrators—but not to the extent that drunk shamings can be labeled as a "male thing." Thus, the culture of alcohol, as illustrated via drunk shaming participation, is not limited to males but also involves females. In some cases females are attempting to compromise the masculinity of a male that they are shaming. One female perpetrator of a drunk shaming stated that she and her girlfriends put an abundance of make-up on a male college athlete (a football player), while he was passed out from consuming too much alcohol. They found it exciting to de-masculinize the football player.

Table 5.2
Perpetrator of a Drunk Shaming by Sex
In Percent

Sex	Yes	No
Male	76	24
Female	47	53

It was suspected that the younger college students are more likely to be involved in drunk shamings than older college students. As one respondent answered in the questionnaire, "acting stupid and writing on your friends because they are drunk is really a high school thing." As this statement implies, there are high school students who not only come to college prepared for the culture of alcohol, they were already indoctrinated into it while in high school. Drunk shamings, however, are not restricted to high school aged students, but, as expected, younger students are more likely to be involved in drunk shamings than older students. More than half (55%) of all the drunk shaming perpetrators were from the 21-23 age group. Thirty-seven percent of the drunk shaming perpetrators were not of legal age (17-20 age category). The remaining eight percent of drunk shaming perpetrators were from the 24-28 age group. As the data in Table 5.3 reveals, the greatest percentage of drunk shamings victims come from 21-23 age group. The second largest percentage of victims come from the underage 17-20 group and twenty-five percent of 24-28 year-old respondents were victims of a drunk shaming (See Table 5.3). In the case of the 24-28 year-olds, the drunk shamings had occurred when the respondents were younger.

Table 5.3
Victim of a Drunk Shaming by Age
In Percent

Age Category	Yes	No
17-20	28	72
21-23	34	66
24-28	25	75
29+	0	100

Respondents were asked to indicate their primary "socialization environment." It was suspected that the culture of alcohol is not restricted to one type of environment (for example, urban over suburban, or rural over urban), but instead, is equally diffused across all socialization environments. All (100%) of the urban and rural respondents had been involved in a drunk shaming in one manner or another and ninety-seven percent of suburban respondents indicated some level of involvement in a drunk shaming. Furthermore, the percentage of victims of drunk shamings was nearly equal across socialization environment categories (See Table 5.4).

As for college residency, nearly all students, on- or off-campus, were equally aware of drunk shamings and had participated at one level or another (perpetrator, victim, or witness). The highest percentage of drunk shaming victims lived off campus but many on-campus and commuter students were also victims of drunk shamings (see Table 5.5).

Table 5.4
Victim of a Drunk Shaming by Socialization Environment
In Percent

Socialization Environment	Yes	No
Urban	28	72
Suburban	31	69
Rural	30	70

The results of college residency and drunk shamings participation rates parallel the age and drunk shaming relationship. That is, the age group most likely to be involved in drunk shamings (21-23) are also more likely to live off-campus than are the youngest age group (17-20) who are more likely to live on-campus (because most colleges require freshman and/or sophomores to live on-campus; unless they are commuters). Further, on-campus students are more likely to have someone in authority (e.g., a Resident Director or Resident Assistant) keeping an eye on their behavior. Obviously, this does not curtail all on-campus and under-aged drinking. Still, drunk shamings are more likely to occur off-campus; and there are a variety of reasons for this. There is less adult supervision of house activities, students live in a group environment that is conducive for any number of housemates picking on other housemates, and there is a great likelihood that most, or all, of the residents are legally old enough to purchase and consumer alcohol.

Table 5.5
Victim of a Drunk Shaming by Residency
In Percent

Residency	Yes	No
On-campus	24	76
Off-campus	46	54
Commuter	30	70

The residency variable may be a little misleading, as drunk shamings do not necessarily occur in the dorms or parental homes of the commuters. Because of this, it is important to examine where the drunk shaming occurs. Based on our research, the highest percentage of drunk shamings occur at off-campus locations such as a friend's home, a student's rented home/apartment, a house party, or other (e.g., outdoor field parties). The lowest percentage of drunk shamings occurs at a bar. It should also be noted that the environment that provides the greatest amount of privacy (a friend's home or one's own home) is the one that is most likely to play host to a drunk shaming. A bar provides the least amount of privacy and therefore is the least likely environment for a drunk shaming. The culture of alcohol helps college students justify their excessive drinking behavior. Mocking drunk friends is a part of this culture. The role of technology has propelled drunk shamings to new levels. People take photos of drunk shaming victims and often post them on the Internet. As one respondent states:

> "The drunk shaming is not complete unless there is a video of the shaming, or at the very least, photos. The shaming has to be posted online as well in order to gain the full effect of a drunk shaming."

Tales From The Drunk Side: "I was throwing up into a bag and peeing in the toilet at the same time."

Undoubtedly, a number of people reading this book have had some experience with drinking to excess or being around someone who has over-indulged at one point or another during their lifetimes. Some readers may have actually been involved with a drunk shaming and can recall their own experiences. Regardless of one's personal experience with drunk shamings, the stories below highlight primary aspects of this element of the culture of alcohol. Let's begin with one male's description of his 22nd birthday:

"I woke up with a jar of peanut butter, a banana with a condom on it in my hand and a shovel was on me."

The respondent could not explain the significance of the shovel but the banana with a condom on it is typical of the pseudo-erotic behavior that is involved with drunk shamings. As another example, a young (17-20) male stated, "I woke up covered in black permanent marker with a penis drawn across my forehead." A male (21-23) had his clothes removed after he passed out and a number of young women placed their breasts and behinds in his face and took photos that were later posted online. Another 21-23-year-old male stated:

I passed out downstairs where everyone was. My friends put another girl's head (who was also passed out) in my lap and placed my hand on her head to make it look like she was going down on me. Then they took pictures and posted them online.

A young male (17-20) describes how he and his friends shamed a buddy of theirs after he passed out drunk at a house party:

We tied him to his weight bench. Then we proceeded to draw lines all over his face. We managed to draw lines on his closed eye balls as well. Next, we drew the word "COCK" in large letters on the side of his face. Then we took photos of him.

In this particular case, the respondent also indicated that the drunk shaming victim was not angry with his friends for trying to embarrass him. This is generally the case with drunk shaming victims.

A female (21-23) drunk shaming victim described how the pseudo-erotic nature of drunk shamings also applies to women in a variety of ways. She indicated that she and her girlfriends look forward to any opportunity to shame guys. In one case, they placed the hands of two guys who had passed out next to each other in each other's crotches. They also wrote "I'm a whore" with a permanent marker on their faces. Another female (21-23) described a drunk shaming involving a male friend who had passed out at a house party: "He fell asleep with his shoes on so me and my girlfriends wrote 'drunk asshole' all over his body." These females were adhering to the drunk shaming rule that anyone who falls asleep with his shoes on is fair game.

In some cases, however, the rules are not adhered to. Such was the case with one respondent who was victimized despite the fact she made it home to her own bed and got her shoes off (which is supposed to save her from being victimized by a drunk shaming):

> "I passed out (with my shoes off, in my own bed) and still got both of my hands colored—one hand was completely blue and the other hand had something written on it... "I love sex" or something to that extent."

A young (17-20) female respondent also referenced the rules and acknowledged why it was "okay" to be victimized:

> "I had passed out with my shoes on. We all know that's against the rules. So, people drew on me with markers and took pictures. I guess I learned my lesson."

Most young people are aware of the "rules" of shaming and recognize that if they do not make it to their own bed and manage to remove their shoes they risk being shamed. An Asian male (21-23) stated:

> "I passed out "with my shoes on" so I got sharpied—written all over my body. "Penis" was written on my forehead and "Made in Korea" on the bottom of my foot. Which, I found 2 weeks later. "

Most drunk shaming victims have things drawn on them or objects placed on them, sometimes in a sexually explicit manner. On other occasions, photos are taken of people who truly have embarrassed themselves. One female (21-23) respondent stated:

> "I was so drunk I wet my pants and my friends set me up on my bed so it was all you could see and [they] took like a half a roll of film/digital pictures."

Another young female (17-20) described an even more embarrassing incident that she endured, that took place in her dorm:

> "I was throwing up into a bag and peeing in the toilet at the same time and my sister took a picture and showed it to people."

Photos are generally taken of the victim so that there is a lasting memory and proof of past behavior. On many occasions these photos are posted online at various drunk shaming sites or personal blogs.

Sample incidents such as the ones described above represent the modern, technological version of drunk shamings. They may also reflect the growing deterioration of morality in society where people no longer feel ashamed for behavior that should bring, at the very least, embarrassment. Alas, most drunk shaming victims simply laugh away any attempts of stigmatization on the part of others.

Drunk Shamings and Self-esteem

Recall that self-esteem refers to one's own positive or negative attitude about the self. People who feel very favorable about themselves are said to have high self-esteem. Conversely, those who possess a very negative self-feeling are said to have low self-esteem. People who fall in the middle of these two categories are said to have moderate self-esteem. Rosenberg's (1965) self-esteem measurement was included in the drunk shaming research questionnaire because this would allow for an examination of drunk shamings based on one's self-esteem level. Respondents were categorized based on a tripartite split leading to categories of high (Rosenberg score 34-40; N=33), moderate (Rosenberg score 30-33; N=38), and low (Rosenberg score 29 and below; N=52) self-esteem.

I was curious as to what effect self-esteem has on drunk shamings. Are people with low self-esteem more likely to be victimized by a drunk shaming or less likely? Are people with low self-esteem less likely to be a perpetrator, more likely to self-shame, more likely to be angry and want revenge when victimized, and are they more likely to gain new insights about themselves as a result of a drunk shaming? Conversely, are people with high self-esteem more likely to be the perpetrators of drunk shamings; less likely to view that their self-esteem was compromised if they are victimized by a drunk shaming; and are they less likely to gain new insights about themselves because of a drunk shaming? These questions are answered below.

Survey Results

At this point, it should be clear that drunk shamings are a quasi-degradation ceremony. As such, they *are* designed to embarrass the "victim." The level of shame experienced by the drunk shaming victim is not equal to that of victims of traditional degradation ceremonies (e.g., court martials and impeachments) because the behavior that led to the shaming is not as serious. Nonetheless, drunk shaming victims may experience great embarrassment and have their shame exposed to a large audience (via an Internet posting). Perpetrators of drunk shamings generally report that the intent of the drunk shaming *is* to embarrass the victim.

In our research, seventy-four percent of respondents agreed (twelve percent strongly agreed) that drunk shamings are meant to embarrass the victim. Further, eighty-one percent of respondents agreed that the drunk shaming victim does experience embarrassment. However, just forty-six percent of respondents agreed that drunk shaming victims feel guilty for their drinking behavior. In contrast, eighty-three percent of drunk shaming victims report that they do not feel guilty for their drinking behavior that led to the drunk shaming; although fifty-two percent agreed that they experienced shame and embarrassment for having their shaming made public. This may be explained by the idea that when embarrassment becomes public, it has meaningful consequences, as others may now condemn the behavior of the embarrassed person (in this case, the drunk shaming victim) (Cupach and Metts, 1992). Twenty-nine percent of victims agreed that they experienced moral indignation as a result of their shaming. Twenty-one percent of drunk shaming victims agreed that they experienced a decrease in self-esteem due to the shaming and nearly the same figure (twenty-five percent) agreed that they felt remorse for their drunken behavior.

So, who is more likely to be a victim of a drunk shaming? Is it someone with high self-esteem or someone with low self-esteem? I had originally thought that people with low self-esteem might be more likely to be victimized by a drunk shaming because twice the percentage of low self-esteem respondents (thirty-seven percent) reported having been told they had a "drinking problem" than did the high self-esteem respondents (eighteen percent). However, as Table 5.6 reveals, respondents with high self-esteem were, surprisingly, nearly as likely as respondents with low self-esteem to be a victim of a drunk shaming. As this data would seem to indicate, people with high self-esteem are just as likely to drink to excess and, therefore, place themselves in a position to be shamed as people with low self-esteem. A respondent with high self-esteem admitted to being kicked out of a bar for being too drunk and then puked outside the bar. His friends took his photo. When he got home, he threw up again before passing out. Again, his friends took his photo. Upon seeing the photos the next day, he simply laughed at his outrageous behavior. A young male with low self-esteem was victimized by a drunk shaming that involved his friends stripping him down to his boxers and then leaving him outside of his dorm room in the dorm hall so that everyone could see him. Initially, he felt embarrassed by the situation but laughed it off a few hours later.

Interestingly, people with moderate self-esteem were the least likely to be a victim of drunk shaming. It is not clear why this is the case.

Table 5.6
Victim of a Drunk Shaming?
In percent, by level of self-esteem

Self-esteem	Yes	No
Low	37	63
Mod	13	87
High	36	64

Perpetrators of drunk shamings, however, were more likely to have high self-esteem. As the data in Table 5.7 reveals, as the level of self-esteem goes up, so to does the percentage of perpetrators. It is believed that people with high self-esteem have a higher level of confidence and therefore are more willing to take the risk of shaming someone. Contrastly, people with low self-esteem may be less likely to shame others for two primary reasons. First, they are worried about the possible retribution from the victim and the fallout that may accompany it. Second, the low self-esteem perpetrator fears being victimized by a drunk shaming in the future. In either case, the low self-esteem perpetrator risks further compromises to his or her sense of self.

Perhaps one of the most fascinating aspects of the culture of alcohol and drunk shaming acceptability is the fact that many people will post photos of their own shaming—in other words, they self-shame. Self-shaming is a clear characteristic of drunk shaming that contrasts it with other degradation ceremonies. As Goffman (1956, 1959) argued, most people attempt to avoid embarrassing situations and degradation ceremonies are designed to embarrass and shame discredited persons.

Table 5.7
Perpetrators of Drunk Shamings
In percent, by level of self-esteem

Self-esteem	Yes	No
Low	43	57
Mod	68	32
High	76	24

Generally, examples of self-shaming in the drunk shaming community involves online posting of photos of "mild content;" such as general drunkenness, being dressed in odd clothing, but no nudity or sexual activity. Self-posting photos on MySpace.com and FaceBook.com has become increasingly popular. People who have their photos posted online risk not only being recognized by others, such as family members, friends, and employers; they also risk being identified by law officials. For example, two men were thrown in jail in April, 2006, after their probation officers found their photos on MySpace. The men posted photos of themselves (self-shaming) holding cups and/or bottles of beer—a violation of their probation! One of the two men was not even of legal age and yet he still posted a photo of himself with beer in hand; clearly, not a wise decision. Shaming such as this goes beyond the realm of drunken inhibition and enters the domain of stupidity.

Self-shaming involves behaviors that deliberately compromise one's sense of self. Consequently, most people will avoid situations that intentionally cause shame and embarrassment to themselves. Thus, people with high self-esteem are more likely to have avoided situations that lead to shame and embarrassment. As a result, it was hypothesized that individuals with low self-esteem were more likely to self-shame than those with high self-esteem. As the data in Table 8 reveals, the percentage of self-shamers increased as the level of self-esteem decreased (See Table 5.8). In the questionnaire, self-shaming respondents were asked to explain why they would purposely shame themselves. Here are some of their responses:

"Drunken photos are fun and the best way to remember what happened the night before."

"I posted a photo of myself with my head in the toilet. I guess some people would see that as shameful but I see it as a sign of a good night out drinking!"

"I've displayed pictures of myself drunk, but I wasn't passed out or really 'shamed.'"

"The photos I have posted online of me drunk are with my friends. We are just having a good time. These photos help to preserve these great moments in time forever. A tell tale sign that I am drunk is that while I am smiling you can see all my teeth and that never happens when I am sober."

In short, the self-shaming photos were viewed more as embarrassing than shameful. I believe that self-shaming behavior by low self-esteem people is an attempt to demonstrate an extroverted character that can be symbolically represented through photos and other recordings (e.g., drunk shaming videos). In this manner, people with low self-esteem are sending a "message" to others that they are having so much fun that they were involved in a "drunk shaming." Projecting this extroverted character through the relative safety of technology to an unknown audience provides distance between the self-shamer and those that view the content. The combination of "mild content" embarrassment and a detached audience are contributing factors for a drunk self-shaming.

Table 5.8
Have you ever self-shamed?
In percent, by level of self-esteem

Self-esteem	Yes	No
Low	27	73
Mod	21	79
High	16	84

As stated previously, the vast majority of perpetrators of drunk shamings express the belief that victims are meant to be embarrassed. However, it has also been revealed that most victims of a drunk shaming do not experience any great embarrassment. As a result, it is unlikely that victims of drunk shamings will experience a compromised sense of self. Why is this the case; especially in light of the fact that many drunk shaming photos are made available to a large audience via an Internet posting? After all, logic would seem to dictate that the larger the audience, the greater the level of embarrassment. However, embarrassment is not as severe when an infraction occurs in front of strangers (regardless of the number of people) as it is when it occurs in front of significant others. Thus, a drunk shaming victim may not feel any great level of embarrassment even if a damaging photo is placed on the Internet (a large audience) if the victim does not believe that his or her significant others (e.g., family members, professors, employer) will view the embarrassing moment of time captured in the form of a drunk shaming.

If anyone is going to be embarrassed enough to have his or her self-esteem compromised as a result of a drunk shaming it would be a safe bet to predict that persons with low self-esteem will suffer the most. The survey results are a bit surprising, in that none of the high or moderate level self-esteem victims reported that their self-esteem was compromised as the result of their shaming. Clearly, these people have managed to simply refuse to acknowledge that their embarrassing behavior is anything to be ashamed of. Experiencing embarrassment, after all, is dependent upon one's socialization. If norm-violators were not socialized to believe that their behavior is worthy of embarrassment (e.g., they don't see anything wrong with being highly intoxicated), they are obviously less likely to experience it. When an embarrassing event such as a drunk shaming occurs, individuals may use a number of strategies in an attempt to restore his/her identity and self-image. In many cases, laughter is a great coping response (Edelmann, 1987). And that is what most drunk shaming victims do— laugh at themselves. Laughing at one's self while others are attempting to mock and embarrass is a good way to defuse a potentially damaging blow to self-esteem. However, it should be noted, that seventeen percent of the low self-esteem victims of a drunk shaming indicated that their self-esteem was compromised (See Table 5.9). For them, simply laughing away their embarrassing moment in time was not a viable option.

Table 5.9
Was your self-esteem compromised as a result of a Drunk Shaming?
In percent, by level of self-esteem

Self-esteem	Yes	No
Low	17	83
Mod	0	100
High	0	100

Seemingly, people with lower self-esteem are more likely to react angrily and want revenge as a result of being victimized by a drunk shaming than those with higher self-esteem. The reasoning is that people with low self-esteem are more sensitive to personal attacks than people with higher self-esteem. The data in Table 10 reveals that a slightly higher percentage of drunk shaming victims with low self-esteem were angry compared to those with high self-esteem but those with moderate self-esteem were the least likely to react angrily (See Table 5.10). It is reasoned that people with low self-esteem are more likely to view a drunk shaming as a threat to their already compromised egos and therefore are more likely to react with anger toward the perpetrators. However, this "logic" does not explain why respondents with high self-esteem were more likely to react with anger than those respondents with moderate self-esteem, or why such a high percentage reacted with anger.

Table 5.10
Were you angry as a result of your drunk shaming?
In percent, by level of self-esteem

Self-esteem	Yes	No
Low	39	61
Mod	29	71
High	33	67

As revealed in this chapter's introductory story, there are times when drunk shaming victims vow revenge. Wanting revenge after being victimized by a degradation ceremony is a common response among victims. After all, an individual's identity has been compromised at the hands of outsiders, some of whom may have a personal vendetta or bias against the victim. That drunk shaming victims would want revenge should not surprise anyone familiar with the criminal justice setting. "Traditionally, in most places throughout the world, restorative justice measures of compensation and restitution have been the dominant model of conflict resolution" (Strang, 2002:3). At the very least, victims generally want justice, some will want material restoration, and others may want an eye-for-an-eye (or tit for tat) style revenge. Wanting revenge is perhaps *the* feature of drunk shamings that most resemble the characteristics of a formal degradation ceremony.

In our research, seventy-three percent of all drunk shaming victims wanted revenge after being victimized by a drunk shaming. Almost predictably, as the level of self-esteem decreased the desire for revenge increased. It should be pointed out; however, that the revenge sought by drunk shaming victims usually comes in the form of a retaliatory shaming (See Table 5.11). Further, most revenge drunk shamings are "good-natured" and meant to be funny—much in the same manner that the initial drunk shamings take place.

Table 5.11
Did you want revenge after being victimized?
In Percent, by level of self-esteem

Self-esteem	Yes	No
Low	78	22
Mod	71	29
High	67	33

There are times when revenge goes too far. In 2006, a 20-year-old man, Travis Maassen, who awoke after a party in La Crosse, Wisconsin and found himself covered in syrup and dry oatmeal (a variation of the "tar and feather" technique) proceeded to pull a gun on his friends who perpetrated the shaming (*The Post-Standard*, 2006). The pranksters were unharmed but Maassen was charged with second-degree recklessly endangering safety while armed. The perpetrators of the shaming told police that they were just trying to "get even" with Maassen for the pranks he had pulled on them in the previous few days.

Shame should trigger self-revelation. Assumingly, drunk shaming victims with low self-esteem would be more likely to gain new insights about themselves compared to those with high self-esteem. This is because people with high self-esteem are less likely to take a drunk shaming as seriously as those with lower self-esteem. Furthermore, the maintenance of self is more important to people with low self-esteem, which would provide more opportunities for them to gain personal insights following a drunk shaming. As the data results shown in Table 5.12 reveal, drunk shaming victims with low self-esteem (thirty-nine percent) were more than twice as likely to have gained new insights about themselves than drunk shaming victims with high self-esteem (seventeen percent) (See Table 5.12). Once again, however, a slight abnormality occurred with the moderate self-esteem group, as they were the least likely to have gained insights about themselves as a result of being victimized by a drunk shaming.

Table 5.12
After being shamed, did you gain new insights about yourself?
In Percent, by level of self-esteem

Self-esteem	Yes	No
Low	39	72
Mod	14	86
High	17	83

The presentation of self is something that is important to humans. Maintaining a positive self-identity involves constant manipulation of the social environment so that others see us in a positive manner. Degradation ceremonies, such as drunk shamings, represent attempts to compromise an individual's sense of self, and consequently, his or her self-esteem. Persons with low self-esteem are especially vulnerable to having their self-esteem compromised as a result of being victimized by a drunk shaming, but they are also more likely to gain new insights about themselves.

Drunk Shamings and Lessons Learned

The culture of alcohol has extended to the realm of public drunk shamings. A drunk shaming is an example of a quasi-degradation ceremony typically perpetrated by friends against friends. Young adults, such as college students, generally find it perfectly acceptable to participate in a culture of alcohol that may lead to a degradation ceremony (a drunk shaming) that is intended to embarrass and bring shame to the drunken victim. However, because of a lack of a permanent stigma attached to being victimized by a drunk shaming, most victims laugh off their embarrassing behavior captured on film and displayed in a public forum. They simply justify their behavior by saying, "I was drunk!"—as if it absolves them of their drunken stupidity. Unlike the Ashanti of the past, in a contemporary court of law, being drunk is not viewed as a justification and ab-solution of irrational behavior. People who drink beyond the legal limit need to keep this in mind—for their own safety and the safety of others.

The fact that some people are willing to post embarrassing photos of them-selves (self-shaming) on the Internet reveals how "normalized" the phenomenon of drunk shamings has become with young people in general, and on college campuses in particular. Clearly, the culture of alcohol is as strong as ever. Tech-nology has further fueled the spreading acceptability of the culture of alcohol to the point where situations that were once deemed embarrassing and shameful are rationalized, dismissed and publicly displayed.

Drunk shamings are visible examples that the culture of alcohol is a very prevalent aspect of popular culture among young adults. In an effort to better understand the drunk shaming culture, participants were asked why they partake in drunk shamings and post embarrassing photos of their friends and themselves on the Internet even though it may cause a loss of self-respect and bring embar-rassment and shame. Here are some of their responses:

> "People react to drunk shamings in different ways. Between myself and my friends, it's a game of fun. It will be something to look at when you're older to get a laugh."

> "Being drunk and doing stupid things happens to everyone once in a while. College is a time for parties and beer."

> I think if you get drunk enough to be shamed, it's your own fault. Also, if your friends shame you, you shouldn't feel bad because they're your friends! If you can't make an ass out of yourself with your friends, who can you make an ass of yourself with?!

Reiterating the idea that drunk shamings are generally meant to be fun deg-radation ceremonies that are not to be taken too seriously, another respondent states:

> "Most shamings do not cause long-term emotional embarrassment. It happens to a lot of people! It's all in fun."

> "Drunk shamings are fun and good times as long as it is done with humor and not too much disrespect."

> "They are meant to be in good fun. If someone gets you, you get them back. It happens to the best of us. Most of the time you know the person well enough to know when and where to draw the line."

> "People I know that have been a "victim" get embarrassed for a short period of time and then just laugh it off, like it wasn't that big of a deal to them."

> "Through my experience, shamings have been done to my friends in good fun and very rarely were feelings hurt."

"Overall, as long as no one is hurt or badly embarrassed, I think most drunk shamings are funny and entertaining."

The fact that most drunk shaming participants view this activity as fun provides credence to the belief that drunk shamings are a quasi-degradation ceremony. Drunk shamings possess some of the critical aspects found in most degradation ceremonies (e.g., personal identity is compromised) but not the more serious ones (e.g., seemingly, there is no permanent compromise to one's sense of self). On the other hand, drunk shamings are also symbolic of the growing culture of shamelessness. Shame reflects morality. And if people no longer experience shame for embarrassing, or deviant, behaviors, then the very fabric of morality may be compromised.

Future research in the area of drunk shamings should involve longitudinal studies where the long-term affects of being victimized by a drunk shaming are examined. In this manner, it would be possible to ascertain whether any permanent damage to one's self-esteem is caused as a result of being victimized by a drunk shaming.

Chapter 6

The Shame of it All!

"The books that the world calls immoral are the books that show the world its own shame"—Oscar Wilde (Irish poet, novelist, and dramatist, 1854-1900)

Have you heard the story involving Richard Gere and his shameful sexual behavior? You know, the one that has been described in media reports as a form of sexual deviance so extreme that it "transgressed all limits of vulgarity." No, not *that* ugly sexually shameful urban legend; rather, the one that involves Gere violating India's strict public obscenity laws. Gere, a friend of the Dalai Lama, the Tibetan spiritual leader, is a frequent visitor to India who promotes awareness of health issues in that nation. On March 15, 2007, Gere appeared with Bollywood star Shilpa Shetty at a public function to bring focus upon India's growing HIV/AIDS incidences.

Bollywood is the informal name used to describe the growing Indian film industry. Bollywood, located in Mumbai, India, is also commonly known as the "Hindi cinema." Shetty, a very attractive actress, is one of Bollywood's biggest stars. She has appeared in nearly fifty films and was crowned the winner of the British *Celebrity Big Brother* in January, 2007.

During the March, 2007 HIV/AIDS awareness event, Gere affectionately hugged and kissed Shetty on stage. While embracing Shetty, Gere romantically bent her down and kissed her several times on the cheek. Photographs of this "incident" were splashed across the front pages of numerous Indian newspapers and caused a public outrage. Crowds in several Indian cities burned effigies of Gere. A New Delhi judge, Dinesh Gupta, declared the kiss vulgar and issued warrants for Gere and Shetty claiming that the couple's public display of affection offended local sensibilities and violated India's strict public obscenity laws. The judge claimed that Gere and Shetty "transgressed all limits of vulgarity and have the tendency to corrupt the society" (*The Post-Standard*, 4/27/07). The judge also criticized Shetty for not resisting Gere's kisses.

Gere acknowledged cultural differences between India and the United States regarding matters of public affection and constructs of obscenity, but insisted that his behavior was not offensive. Shetty also remained unrepentant. She argued that the negative reactions sparked by her shameless behavior with Gere do not reflect the views of the vast majority of Indians. She expressed concern whether Gere would come back to her country to help promote future causes.

As the Gere-Shetty story reveals, shifting cultural attitudes regarding "proper" behavior are not unique to the United States. In fact, much of the world is coming to grips with altering ideals.

Shamelessness Meets Resistance

The focus of this book has been to demonstrate the cultural change in Americans' attitudes regarding "shameful" behaviors. As demonstrated in chapter 1, the labeling of certain behaviors as shameful has always been tied to constructs of morality. Early ethos of American morality were influenced by the Puritan ethic and, later, by the idea that one must not succumb to the "Seven Deadly Sins." Morality itself is influenced by cultural norms and values. As the norms and values of a society change, notions of morality also change. Correspondingly, behaviors that are labeled as shameless or shameful will be adjusted to fit the current cultural stance. Thus, at any given time—and seemingly, especially at the present—a growing culture of shamelessness is likely to emerge as new cultural norms surface. Often, as new cultural norms arise, older members of any given society are likely to put up a challenge. The old guard will employ any method possible to stop the emergence of a growing culture of shamelessness. Among the weapons at their disposal are embarrassment and shame.

Embarrassment and shame are primary components of formal shamings. Formal shamings are discussed in chapter 2. Sociologically speaking, formal shamings are degradation ceremonies that are designed to compromise the offender's sense of self, self-esteem, and self-identity. Most people attempt to keep intact a positive sense of self because, well, it is good for our self-esteem! Educators have long promoted the value of self-esteem. In many cases, social policy makers have gone overboard in their attempt to keep a fragile person's self-esteem at an elevated level. For example, years ago, it became common to give all youth participants in sports or some school event a trophy. Not just the winners, but the losers too. After all, even if you lose, you're a winner! Unless we're talking about the Special Olympics, let's reserve trophy presentations to those who earn them.

Because people are generally concerned about their sense of self, they will seek to avoid situations that may compromise their self-esteem. Consequently, avoiding a formal shaming should be a top concern for the majority of people. Degradation ceremonies not only shame individuals, they stigmatize them. A military court martial is perhaps the best example of a formal degradation ceremony, but lately an increasing number of judicial shamings have sprung up across the United States. As court-ordered shamings reveal, we are not going further away from the Puritan days of public humiliations via the stocks and the wearing of a Scarlet "A;" we are, instead, nearing a return to such an era. Judicial shamings are a clear indicator that the culture of shamelessness is being met with resistance. After all, the primary purpose of a judicial shaming is to bring humiliation and embarrassment upon the offender.

Resistance also comes in the shape of informal shamings. As described in chapter 3, informal shamings may be viewed as quasi-degradation ceremonies. Like formal degradation ceremonies, informal shamings contain rudiments of moral indignation, shame, stigmatism, and embarrassment. However, unlike formal degradation ceremonies, informal shamings are not conducted in an official capacity by some social institution. Instead, they are instituted by family members, friends, peer groups, and other "unofficial" associates. Not surprisingly, in this growing culture of shamelessness, many people find joy in shaming others. Pulling pranks and April Fool's Day jokes on others are examples of informal shamings. The media, lovers scorned, musicians, and athletes are among those who conduct informal shamings.

In chapter 4, the fascinating concept of self-shaming was explored. One's willingness to self-shame is a clear indicator of a growing culture of shamelessness. After all, historically speaking, most people have routinely attempted to avoid situations that purposively bring shame and embarrassment. Today, however, people engage in all sorts of self-shaming behaviors. They will express extreme forms of individuality despite constant ridicule from society; they will post embarrassing photos and retell shameful stories of themselves on online journals and websites; try out for singing competitions even though they have no singing talent; and engage in unhealthy self-shaming behaviors such as self-hatred, eating disorders, and self-mutilations. The fact that so many people are no longer ashamed of behaviors, which in the past would be labeled as shameful, is indeed a sign of a growing culture of shamelessness.

Most likely, we have all engaged in some sort of behavior that left us feeling embarrassed, and perhaps, even ashamed. Unless we are self-shamers, we prefer that these moments of lapses of proper judgment remain buried, or at the very least, that the knowledge of these events be limited to the participants actually involved. Go ahead and ask yourself this question: "Have you ever done something you regret, and was alcohol involved?" It seems that alcohol, the drug that helps to release inhibitions, is often associated with shameful behaviors. As detailed in chapter 5, young people often find joy in further humiliating their drunken friends. They will use a permanent marker and draw stuff on the body of their "fallen" comrades. They may also place objects on/near the victim, expose the victim by taking his/her clothing off, shave the eyebrows and/or hair, and rearrange the victim's body into embarrassing bodily positions. In short, they commit a drunk shaming.

Drunk shamings are meant to embarrass and shame a person who drinks too much and then passes out. Although this ritual has been conducted for generations, the current younger generation has the Internet at its disposal to embarrass the drunk person in front of a large audience. Interestingly, there are people willing to self-shame by posting drunk shaming photos of themselves online. Think about it. People are actually willing to post embarrassing photos of themselves online. These self-shamers usually laugh it off. However, the participants of the growing culture of shamelessness need to realize that the forces of resistance also include potential future employers who may have also viewed these photos and found them to be shameful, not shameless.

It is clear there is a growing culture of shamelessness developing in the United States. But it is also apparent that there are cultural forces of resistance to assure that the morality of society does not disappear completely. My own reflections as to why our society is becoming more shameless were provided throughout the book. Perhaps the most overwhelming explanation rests with the younger generation's desire to become popular and famous, at any cost. Thus, in an attempt to gain, at minimum, "15 minutes of fame," an increasing number of people are willing to violate traditional rules, norms, values, and etiquette expectations.

Implications for the Future

So what does the future hold for us? No one knows for sure, of course. It seems like the standards adhered to by adults are ignored by the younger generation. And perhaps that is partially true. But there are two points worth considering. First, every generation complains about the attitudes and behaviors of the younger generation. I like to share this quote with my freshmen college students: "Teenagers these days are out of control. They eat like pigs, they are disrespectful of adults, they interrupt and contradict their parents, and they terrorize their teachers." I then ask my students, "Who said this?" One semester, a young woman replied, "An old dude?" The class burst out in laughter. And, I must admit, I too, found her response to be funny. After all, it *was* an old dude. His name was Aristotle and the quote was attributed to him in 350 B.C.! Clearly, the notion that the younger generation pays little attention to the rules and expectations of the older generation is nothing new. Undoubtedly, the "rebels" of youth of this generation expect that older folks should accept their ideals and, further, that these new ideals should become the new standard of morality. Won't these young people be surprised when the next generation, yet to be born, rises to challenge these newly formed standards?

The second point worth considering is, perhaps, more substantial. That is, even in the growing culture of shamelessness, there are still plenty of examples of shameful behaviors that members of a moral community agree on. For example, because no one wants to be a victim of an assault, especially the heinous crime of rape, violent acts of aggression perpetrated by one person(s) against another person(s) will always be deemed shameful. Any crime committed against a child is particularly shameful. Child abuse is especially immoral and heart-wrenching. Further, no one wants to be a victim of any type of crime. For example, when we return to our homes after working or attending some sort of event, we expect that our possessions will still be there. People who are burglarized do not employ the drunk shaming attitude of, "Well, it's okay, as long as the burglars were drunk. We can excuse theft when it is alcohol-related." No! We do not want to be victimized by a crime at any time. In fact, utilizing the excuse that crime is okay as long as the criminals were drunk is as ridiculous as justifying non-criminal behaviors just because someone was drunk.

Although many people shamelessly cheat on their significant others, in nearly all cases, we find it shameful when our significant other cheats on us. It is especially shameful if someone leaves his or her spouse after discovering that he or she has a crippling or fatal disease. A person who leaves a spouse returning from war because he or she has lost limbs is particularly shameful.

In recent years, there have been many documented cases (including videos shown on You Tube) of assailants beating up homeless people and extremely old people. This is clearly shameful behavior, as homeless people are seldom in a position to defend themselves. What possible benefit can anyone gain from beating up a homeless person? We can expand this idea to label all examples of violence against humans and animals as shameful. Purposively harming the environment is also shameful. Littering, for example, is a prime example of shameful behavior. Most likely we have all witnessed people shamelessly throwing objects, like fast-food wrappers and cigarette butts, out their car windows. Why do they do this? Do they possess some sense of self-entitlement that allows them to break the law and make the world a less-attractive place to reside? That people can so callously violate basic norms of decency is clearly a reflection of the growing culture of shamelessness.

Emotional abuse, such as making fun of the less fortunate, is also shameful. Emotional abuse against family members and other loved ones is shameful behavior. Talking poorly about a friend or loved one behind his or her back is shameful. Racism, sexism, ageism, and nearly all of the isms are examples of shameful behaviors.

A Parting Thought

It has been established that an increasing number of people are shamelessly participating in behaviors that were once labeled shameful. The movie *Phone Booth* provides us with a subtle difference in perception when it was pointed out that it used to be a sign of insanity to talk to oneself, but now, because of hand free cell phones, it is a sign of status.

Nonetheless there are vanguards of morality who are prepared to label others' shameless behavior as shameful. Thus, even though people are free to shamelessly post photos, even drunk ones or sexually explicit ones, of themselves on homepages of various Internet sites, they need to be prepared for the possible negative consequences. For example, people who post drunk photos of themselves online may find this shameless, but if drinking violates the conditions of their probation and their probation officer views these photos, the violators may shamefully find themselves in jail. Similarly, a young person who shamelessly posts drunk or risqué photos of herself on her Facebook page risks not getting a desired job if a potential employer views those photos. Further, it is only natural for young people to challenge the norms and values of the older generation. Generally, finding some sort of middle ground is best for all concerned. After all, any one of us is capable of shamelessly participating in a behavior that may be labeled as shameful. And there appears to be a great number of people out there just waiting to capture it on film, and post it online.

It's not just "Big Brother" who is watching; it's everybody and their brother!

Bibliography

ABC.com. 2007. "*America's Funniest Home Videos.*" Available:
   Http://abc.go.com/primetime/AmericasFunniest/show.html.
American Academy of Family Physicians. 2006. "Eating Disorders: Facts and
   Teens."
   Available: http://familydoctor.org/277.
Arrighi, Barbara A. 1997. *America's Shame*. Westport, CT: Praeger.
Asendorpf, J. 1984. "Shyness, Embarrassment, and Self-presentation: A Control
   Theory Approach," pp. 109-114 in *The Self in Anxiety, Stress, and De-
   pression*, edited by R. Schwarzer. Amsterdam: North Holland.
Aviv, Rachel. 2007. "Black Tie (and Pants) Optional." *The Post-Standard*,
   January 8: D-2.
Baum, Lawrence. 2006. Judges and Their Audiences: A Perspective in *Judicial
   Behavior*. Princeton, NJ: Princeton University Press.
Brothers, Joyce. 2005. "Shame May Not Be So Bad After All," in *Parade*, Feb-
   ruary 27:4, 6-7.
Buss, A. H. 1980. *Self-Consciousness and Social Anxiety*. San Francisco: W.H.
   Freeman.
Cast, Alicia D. and Peter J. Burke. 2002. "A Theory of Self-Esteem." *Social
   Forces*, 80:1041-1068.
Chappelle, Dave. 2004. *Showtime* comedy special, "For What It's Worth."
Chicago Tribune (online edition). 2007. "McDonald's Fights 'McJob.'" March
   21.
Cobb, N.J. 2001. *Adolescence: Continuity, Change, and Diversity* (4th ed.).
   Mountain View, CA: Mayfield Publishing Company.
Coin, Glenn. 2005. "Colleges Stricter on Alcohol Policies." *The Post-Standard*.
   October, 24:A-1.
Congressional Research Service. 2004. "CRS Report for Congress: Military
   Courts-Martial: An Overview." May 26, Order Code: RS21850.
Cooney, Ned L., Ronald M. Kadden, and Howard R. Steinberg. 2005. "Assess-
   ment of Alcohol Problems," pp. 71-112 in *Assessment of Addictive
   Behaviors*, 2nd edition, Edited by Dennis M. Donovan and G. Alan
   Marlatt. New York: Guilford.
Copeland, Libby. 2005. "Shaming Drunks is a College Fad," in *The Post-
   Standard*. January 23:H-1.

Crow, R. Brian and Scott R. Posner. 2004. "Hazing and Sport and the Law,"
      pp.200-223 in *The Hazing Reader*, edited by Hank Nuwer. Blooming-
      ton, IN: Indiana University Press.
Crocker, Jennifer, Shawna J. Lee and Lora E. Park. 2004. "The Pursuit of Self-
      esteem: Implications for Good and Evil," pp. 271-302 in *The Social
      Psychology of Good And Evil*, edited by Arthur G. Miller. New York:
      Guilford.
Cupach, W.R. and S. Metts. 1992. "The Effects of Type of Predicament and
      Embarrassability on Remedial Responses to Embarrassing Situations.
      Communication Quarterly, 40:149-161.
Cuzzort, R. P. and Edith W. King. 1995. *Twentieth-Century Social Thought*, 5th
      edition. Fort Worth, TX: Harcourt Brace.
Davenport, Noa, Ruth Distler Schwartz, and Gail Pursell Elliott. 2005. Mob-
      bing: *Emotional Abuse in the American Workplace*, 3rd edition. Ames,
      IA: Civil Society Publishing.
Debernardi, Jean. 2004. *Rites of Belonging*. Stanford, CA: Stanford University
      Press.
Delaney, Tim. 2004. *Classical Social Theory: Investigation and Application*.
      Upper Saddle River, NJ: Pearson/Prentice Hall.
_____. 2005. *Contemporary Social Theory*. Upper Saddle River, NJ:
      Pearson/Prentice Hall.
_____. 2006. *Seinology: The Sociology of Seinfeld*. Amherst, NY: Prome-
      theus.
_____. 2008. *Simpsonology: There's a Little Bit of Springfield in All of Us*.
      Amherst, NY: Prometheus.
Delaney, Tim and Patrick Tanzini. 2005. Original Drunk Shamings research.
Deveny, Kathleen and Raina Kelley. 2007. "Girls Gone Wild: What Are The
      Celebs Teaching Kids?" Available: Http://www.msnbc.msn.com.
Durkheim, Emile. 1933 [1895]. *The Rules of Sociological Method*. New York:
      Free Press.
Egelko, Bob. 2004. "Shaming Ok'd As Part of Sentence. Court Upholds Thief's
      Wearing 'I Stole Mail' Sign." *San Francisco Chronicle*, August 10:
      B4.
Edelmann, Robert J. 1987. *The Psychology of Embarrassment*. New York:
      Wiley & Sons.
FOX News.com. 2007 "Judge Says Illinois Man Can't Change Name to Peyton
      Manning." March 28. Available at: http://www.foxnews.com.
Garfinkel, Harold. 1956. "Conditions of Successful Degradation Ceremonies."
      American Journal of Sociology, 61:420-424.
Gecas, Viktor and Peter J. Burke. 1995. "Self and Identity," pp. 41-67 in *Socio-
      logical Perspectives on Social Psychology*, edited by K.S. Cook, G.A.
      Fine, and J.S. House. Boston: Allyn and Bacon.
Gilligan, James. 1996. *Violence: Our Deadly Epidemic and Its Causes*. New
      York: Putnam.

Glidden-Tracey, Cynthia E. 2005. *Counseling and Therapy with Clients Who Abuse Alcohol or Other Drugs: An Integrative Approach.* Mahwah, NJ: Lawrence Erlbaum.

Goffman, Erving. 1956. "Embarrassment and Social Organization." *American Journal Of Sociology.* 62 (3): 264-271.

_____. 1959. *The Presentation of Self in Everyday Life.* Garden City, NY: Anchor.

_____. 1963A. *Behavior In Public Places: Notes on the Social Organization of Gatherings.* Glencoe, IL: Free Press.

_____. 1963B. *Stigma: Notes on the Management of a Spoiled Identity.* Englewood Cliffs, NJ: Prentice Hall.

Gruenewald, Tara L., Margaret E. Kemeny, Najib Aziz, and John L. Fahey. 2004. "Acute Threat to the Social Self: Shame, Social Self-esteem, and Cortisol Activity." *Psychosomatic Medicine,* 66:915-924.

Halpern, Jake. 2006. Fame Junkies: *The Hidden Truths Behind America's Favorite Addiction.* Boston: Houghton-Mifflin.

Hart, Kim. 2006. "Angry Customers Use Web to Shame Firms." *Washington Post.* July 5: D-1.

Hines, Thomas. 2002. *I Want That: How We All Became Shoppers.* New York: Perennial.

Hoebel, E. Adamson. 1964. *The Law of Primitive Man: A Study in Comparative Legal Dynamics.* Cambridge, MA: Harvard University Press.

Hoffman, Claire. 2006. "Joe Francis: 'Baby, Give Me a Kiss.'" *Los Angeles Times*, August 6. Available: http://www.latimes.com/features/magaizne/west.

International Labour Office. 2003. "Alcohol and Drug Problems at Work: The Shift to Prevention." International Labour Office: Geneva, Switzerland.

James, Wendy. 2003. *The Ceremonial Animal.* Oxford: University Press.

Jaret, Charles, Donald C. Reitzes, and Nadezda Shapkina. 2005. "Reflected Appraisals And Self-Esteem." *Sociological Perspectives,* 48(3):403-419.

Jayson, Sharon. 2006. "Are Social Norms Steadily Unraveling?" *USA Today,* April 13: 4D.

_____. 2007. "Generation Y's Goal? Wealth and Fame." *USA Today,* January 1.

Johnson, L.A. 2007. "How Tacky Can We Get?" *Pittsburgh Post-Gazette* (as appeared in *The Post-Standard*), May 20: I-1, I-2).

Jones, E.E. and T.S. Pittman. 1982. "Toward a General Theory of Strategic Self-Presentation," pp. 231-262 in *Psychological Perspectives on the Self,* (Vol.1), edited by J. Suls. Hillsdale, NJ: Lawrence Erlbaum.

Keveney, Bill. 2007. "'Idol' Insults Give Rejects a Claim to Fame." *USA Today,* January 23: 1D.

Lang, Alan R. 1992. *The Encyclopedia of Psychoactive Drugs: Alcohol and Teenage Drinking,* introduction by Jack H. Mendelson and Nancy K. Mello. New York: Chelsea House.

Leary, M. R. and R. M. Kowalski. 1990. "Impression Management: A Literature Review and Two-Component Model." *Psychological Bulletin*, 107:34-47.

Lederman, Linda C. and Lea P. Stewart. 2005. *Changing the Culture of College Drinking: A Socially Situated Health Communication Campaign.* Cresskill, NJ: Hampton Press.

Lerner, R.M., Freund, A.M., De Stefanis, I., Habermas, T. 2001. Understanding Developmental Regulation in Adolescence: The Use of the Selection, Optimization and Compensation Model. *Human Development*, 44, 29-50.

Lewis, Michael. 1998. "Shame and Stigma," pp. 126-140 in *Shame: Interpersonal Behavior, Psychopathology, and Culture*, edited by Paul Gilbert and Bernice Andrews. New York: Oxford University Press.

Leymann, Heinz. 1990. "Mobbing and Psychological Terror at Workplaces." *Violence And Victims*, 5(2):119-126.

_____. 1996. "The Content and Development of Mobbing at Work." *European Journal of Work and Organizational Psychology.* 5(2):165-184.

Lindersmith, Alfred R., Anselm L. Strauss and Norman K. Denzin. 1991. *Social Psychology*, 7th edition. Englewood Cliffs, NJ: Prentice Hall.

Los Angeles Times. 2006. "Montana: Man Must Wear 'I Am Not a Marine' Sign." July 8: A19.

MacAndrew, Craig and Robert B. Edgerton. 1969. *Drunken Comportment*. New York: Aldine.

Maguire, Marti. 2007. "DWIs Get Shaming: Group Works To Lower Hispanics' Rate." *The News & Observer* (Raleigh, NC). March 8.

McKenzie, John L. 1965. *Dictionary of the Bible*. Milwaukee: Bruce Publishing.

Mead, G. H. 1934. Mind, Self & Society, edited and with an introduction by Charles W. Morris. Chicago: University of Chicago Press.

Miller, Rowland S. 1996. *Embarrassment: Poise and Peril in Everyday Life.* New York: Guilford Press.

Morris, Meaghan. 2006. *Identity Anecdotes: Translation and Media Culture.* Thousand Oaks, CA: Sage.

Mruk, Christopher J. 1999. *Self-esteem*, 2nd edition. New York: Springer.

MSNBC. 2007. "High Court Gets 'Bong Hits 4 Jesus' Case." Available at: http://www.msnbc.msn.com.

Museum of Hoaxes. 2007. "Top 100 April Fool's Day Hoaxes of All Time." Available at: http://www.museumofhoaxes.com/hoax/aprilfool

Nixon II, Howard L. and James H. Frey. 1996. *A Sociology of Sport*. Belmont, CA: Wadsworth.

Patrick, Clarence H. 1952. *Alcohol, Culture, and Society*. Durham, NC: Duke University Press.

Parker, Kathleen. 2007. "Watching Saddam's Death was a Twisted Pleasure." *The Post-Standard*. January 8: A-8.

Phinney, J.S. 2000. Identity Formation across Cultures: The Interaction of Personal, Societal and Historical Change. *Human Development*, 43, 27-31.

Ratt. 1990. Lyrics to "Shame, Shame, Shame," from *Detonator*, Atlantic Records.

Real, Michael R. 1996. *Exploring Media Culture: A Guide*. Thousand Oaks, CA: Sage.

Redhage, Jill. 2006. "County Tries to Deter DUIs With Ads: Mug Shots of Offenders Will Go Up On Internet Site." *The Tribune* (Meza, AZ). December 14.

Reilly, Rick. 2006. "Here's the *Real* Crime." *Sports Illustrated*, August 29:72.

Rosenberg, Morris. 1965. *Society and the Adolescent Self-Image*. Princeton, NJ: Princeton University Press.

Ritzer, George. 1993. *The McDonaldization of Society*. Newbury Park, CA: Pine Forge Press.

_____. 2002. "McJobs: McDonaldization and its Relationship to the Labor Process," pp. 141-147 in *McDonaldization: The Reader*, edited by George Ritzer. Thousand Oaks, CA: Pine Forge Press.

Rubinstein, Robert L. and Kate de Medeiros. 2005. "Home, Self, and Identity," pp. 47-62 in *Home and Identity in Late Life*, edited by Graham D. Rowles and Habib Chaudhury. New York: Springer.

Ruyter, D.D., Conroy, J. 2002. The Formation of Identity: The Importance of Ideals. *Oxford Review of Education*, 28(4), 509-522.

Schlenker, B.R. 1980. *Impression Management: The Self-Concept Social Identity and Interpersonal Relations*. Monterey, CA: Brooks/Cole.

Schlenker, B. R. and M. R. Leary. 1982. "Social Anxiety and Self-presentation: A Conceptualization and Model. *Psychological Bulletin*. 92: 641-669.

Schreiner, Bruce. 2005. "Amish Shunning Runs Afoul of Law." November 5. Available:
http://www.deitscherei.org/gewebblog/20051122142902.html.

Seinfeld. 1991. "The Deal," episode #14. First aired on May 2, 1991.

_____. 1992. "The Pez Dispenser," episode #31. First aired on January 15, 1992.

_____. 1995. "The Face Painter," episode #109. First aired on May 11, 1995.

Shannon, Elaine and Ann Blackman. 2002. *The Spy Next Door*. Boston: Little & Brown.

Shipman, Tim. 2006. "A Public Shaming For Child Support Dodgers," *Daily Mail*. December 11: 20.

Shu-fang Dien, D. S. 2000. The Evolving Nature of Self-Identity Across Four Levels of History. *Human Development*, 43, 1-18.

Simon, Carly. 1972. Lyrics to "You're So Vain," from *No Secrets*.

Snyder, Eldon E. and Elmer Spreitzer. 1978. *Social Aspects of Sport*. Englewood Cliffs, NJ: Prentice Hall.

Strang, Heather. 2003. *Repair or Revenge?* Oxford: Clarendon.

Stephens, R. Todd. 2004. "Knowledge: The Essence of Meta Data: Six Degrees of Separation of Our Assets." September 16. Available:
http://www.dmreview.com

Stone, Brad. 2006. "MySpace Turned Music Fandom Into Gold." *Newsweek*. Available: http://www.msnbc.msn.com/id/8682505/site/newsweek/

Stryker, Sheldon and Richard T. Serpe. 1994. "Identity Salience and Psycho-
      logical Centrality: Equivalent, Overlapping, or Complementary Con-
      cepts?" *Social Psychology Quarterly*, 57:16-35.
Swinford, Steven and Daniel Foggo. 2006. "'Lenient' Judges Shamed in List."
      The Sunday Times. June 11: 1.
The Economist. 2006. "Ingenious Punishments: Their Object All Sublime." Oc-
      tober 14:31.
The Holy Bible: King James Version. 2000. "The First Epistle of Paul the Apos-
      tle to Timothy 3."
The Post-Standard. 2005. "Did You See?" June 4: A-2.
_____. 2006. "Did You See?" March 16: A-2.
_____. 2006. "Survey: Americans Biggest Patriots." June, 28: A-13.
_____. 2007. "8-Year-Old Girl Allegedly Made 135 Fake 911 Calls." Febru-
      ary 10: A-8.
_____. 2007. "Keith Richards Admits He Couldn't Resist Snorting His Fa-
      ther's   Ashes." April 4: A-2.
_____. 2007. "Richards: Story Was a Joke." April 5: A-2.
_____. 2007. "Did You See?" April 6: A-2.
_____. 2007. "India Orders Arrest of Richard Gere for Kiss." April 27:E-3.
_____. 2007. "Thai Police who Break the Rules Will Wear 'Hello Kitty'
      Armbands as Punishment." August 7: A-2.
_____. 2007. "Video Creator Not Giving Up." October 26: A-2.
The Simpsons. 1990. "Dancin' Homer," episode #18 (7F05). First aired on No-
      vember 8, 1990.
_____. 1991. "One Fish, Two Fish, Blowfish, Blue Fish," episode #24
      (7F11). First aired on January 24, 1991.
_____. 1991. "Principal Charming," episode #27 (7F15). First aired on Feb-
      ruary 14, 1991.
_____. 1991. "When Flanders Failed," episode #38 (7F23). First aired on
      October 3, 1991.
_____. 1995. "The Springfield Connection," episode #126 (2F21). First
      aired on May 7, 1995.
_____. 2005. "There's Something About Marrying," episode #345
      (GABF04). First aired on February 20, 2005.
The Sun. 2006. "Sun Campaign: Judges on Trial." June 12: 3, 8-9.
Twenge, Jean M. 2006. *Generation Me*. New York: Free Press.
U.S. Department of Health and Human Services (Office on Women's Health).
      2007. "Eating Disorders." Available at: www.4Women.gov.
USA Today. 2004. "Shame Works, So Use It." September 1: 14A.
Veblen, Thorstein. 1934 [1899]. *The Theory of the Leisure Class: An Economic
      Study of Institution*, with a Foreword by Stuart Chase. New York: Ran-
      dom House. Bacon.
Walters, Scott T. and John S. Baer. 2006. *Talking with College Students About
      Alcohol: Motivational Strategies for Reducing Abuse*. New York: Guil-
      ford.

Wechsler, Henry and Bernice Wuethrich. 2002. *Dying to Drink: Confronting Binge Drinking on College Campuses.* New York: Rodale.

Weitzman, E. R., T. F. Nelson, and H. Wechsler. 2003. "Taking up Binge Drinking in College: The Influences of Person, Social Group, and Environment." *Journal of Adolescent Health,* 32:26-35.

Whitman, James Q. 2003. *Harsh Justice: Criminal Punishment and Widening Divide Between America and Europe.* New York: Oxford University Press.

Zernike, Kate. 2005. "Failed Abu Ghraib Plea Reveals Breakups, Betrayals." *The New York Times.* May 10. Available: http://aolsvc.news.aol.com/news/article.adp.

Index

About the Author

Tim Delaney teaches sociology, popular culture, and criminology courses at the State University of New York at Oswego. He earned his Ph.D. in sociology from the University of Nevada Las Vegas; M.A. in sociology from California State University Dominquez Hills, and B.S. in sociology, with a psychology minor, from the State University of New York at Brockport. Delaney has authored numerous books, book chapters, and articles. Among his published books are: *Simpsonology: There's a Little Bit of Springfield In All of Us!* (2008), *Seinology: The Sociology of Seinfeld* (2006), *American Street Gangs* (2006), *Contemporary Social Theory: Investigation and Application* (2005), and *Classical Social Theory: Investigation and Application* (2004). Delaney also serves as a "media expert" and is often quoted in newspapers and interviewed on radio and television. Learn more about Tim Delaney at his website: www.BooksByTimDelaney.com.